POCKET

ROTTERDAM

TOP SIGHTS · LOCAL EXPERIENCES

D0949043

VIRGINIA MAXWELL

Contents

Plan Your Trip 4

Markthal (p40)
OSCITY/SHUTTERSTOCK ©

Special Features

Welcome to Rotterdam

Innovation is the mantra in the Netherlands' second-biggest city and the locals embrace it with unbridled enthusiasm. It's not just the cutting-edge architecture and urban design present in every neighbourhood that make the city special – although the design culture here really *is* extraordinary. Instead, it's the general willingness to try anything once – be it different foods, outré artistic experiences, new-wave coffee or pretty well anything else.

Erasmusbrug (p89) and Wilhelminapier
PETER DE KIEVITH/SHUTTERSTOCK ©

Top Sights

Van Nelle Fabriek

Architecturally resplendent 1930s factory complex. **p66**

Huis Sonneveld

Outstanding example of Dutch Functionalism. **p34**

Museum Rotterdam '40-'45 NU

Multimedia stories about war and resistance. **p68**

Kinderdijk

Unesco-listed windmill landscape. **p136**

Vermeer Centrum Delft

Celebrating Vermeer's art and life. **p100**

Mauritshuis

Dutch Golden Age treasure trove. **p114**

Escher in Het Paleis

Celebration of unorthodox graphic design. **p116**

Gouda

The perfect, cheesy litle town. **p138**

Eating

Forget fine dining – Rotterdammers don't like formality and fuss, and are at their happiest when enjoying fresh, seasonally driven, cafe-style food. The city is replete with informal restaurants and also has two great food markets – Markthal and Fenix Food Factory – that have eateries alongside produce stalls.

Global Accents

Contemporary Dutch cuisine has been significantly influenced by the country's colonial past, with Indonesian and Surinamese dishes and flavours appearing on many local menus. In Rotterdam, these and other global cuisines are represented not just in dedicated restaurants but within the eclectic menus of cafes across the city, which are just as likely to offer buddha bowls and falafel as they are the Dutch staples of cheese sandwiches and apple pie.

Fresh is Best

Be sure to visit Rotterdam's two main food markets: the architecturally resplendent Markthal (pictured; p40) and ultra-hip Fenix Food Factory (p90). Both are hybrid shopping and eating venues where you can buy fresh seasonal and artisanal produce – everything from freshly baked sourdough to meats, freshly roasted coffee beans and a huge array of Gouda cheese. To source organic produce, head to the De Groene Passage (p52) eco-emporium.

Best Breakfasts

Rolph's Deli All-day breakfasts including bagels and *broodjes* (bread rolls) with multiple toppings. (p92)

Pierre Flakey, buttery croissants and perfect *croque monsieurs*. (p45)

Bertmans Treats including *pannenkoekjes* (pancakes), avocado toast and a delicious fruit crumble. (p59)

Man Met Bril The city's best-value breakfast deal and most impressive coffee (p62)

Hopper Artisan bakery cafe serving delectable pastries and above-average coffee. (p47)

Picknick Home to the famous 'Picknick platters'. (p48)

KIEV.VICTOR/SHUTTERSTOCK ©

Best Cafe Lunches

Urban Espresso Bar The burger, soup and salad of the day are always worth checking out. (p75)

Hopper Sensational sandwiches, hearty soups and coffee made with house-roasted beans. (p47)

Parqiet Enjoy freshly made sandwiches and salads in leafy Het Park. (p77)

Best Dinner Venues

Aji Small plates with loads of flavour. (p45)

CEO Baas van Het Vlees The best steaks in the city. (p91)

HMB Sleek restaurant serving sophisticated, beautifully presented contemporary cuisine. (p91)

Asian Glories Modern rifts on Chinese classics. (p47)

FG Flagship restaurant of Rotterdam's superstar chef François Geurds. (p61)

Zeezout Ultrafresh global seafood dishes. (p47)

Best Sweet Treats

Dudok Home to the city's best apple pie. (p47)

Urban Bakery Rotterdam's best cupcakes and brownies. (p61)

Lof der Zoetheid Lavish and delicious high tea, complete with samovar. (p59)

De IJsmaker Freshly churned, supersmooth gelato in fruit, nut and chocolate flavours. (p46)

Koen Authentic Italian-style gelato made fresh daily. (p62)

Best Pizza

O'Pazzo Neapolitan-style pizzas served in family-friendly surrounds. (p47)

Angelo Betti Crispy pizzas and damn fine gelato. (p60)

Drinking & Nightlife

Locals are equally enamoured of coffee and beer, and can be convinced to enjoy an expertly made cocktail too. There's no lack of cafes, cocktail bars, microbreweries and pubs – many with outdoor seating for summer – and these are scattered across town. Witte de Withstraat is the main bar street.

Coffee Craze

Since local coffee roastery Man Met Bril (p62) started sourcing and roasting direct-trade beans in 2012, the city has embraced artisan coffee culture with alacrity. There are now 12 roasteries supplying cafes across the city, and the quality of the coffee these cafes serve is among the best in the country. Not all of the roasteries have their own cafes (two that do are Man Met Bril and Hopper; p47), but freshly roasted beans by local companies including Giraffe are being used in coffee machines across the city and South Holland, and the results are well worth sampling.

Microbreweries

When the locals aren't sipping coffee made with locally roasted coffee beans, they're more than likely to be enjoying a locally brewed beer at one of the city's growing number of microbreweries. Seasonal and standard beers are usually on offer, and some microbreweries offer new customers tasting flights to introduce their tipples. In summer, the outdoor terraces of these places are the most popular drinking destinations in town.

Best Cafes

Man Met Bril Mecca for serious coffee drinkers; beans don't come any fresher. (p62)

Urban Espresso Bar Giraffe beans, expert baristas and top-notch cafe food. (p75)

Hopper Roasts its own beans and makes sensational sandwiches. (p47)

Lokaal Uses Giraffe beans to make espresso and filter brews. (p63)

IRIS VAN DEN BROEK/SHUTTERSTOCK ©

Best Microbreweries

Kaapse Brouwers Great location in the Fenix Food Factory on the banks of the Maas river. (p92)

Stadsbrouwerij De Pelgrim Canalside seating and signature Mayflower Tripel brew. (p79)

Eurotrash United Student and artist hang-out, with beer almost as good as the brewery's name. (p62)

Brouwerij Noordt In the happening Noord neighbourhood; 20 tipples on tap. (p62)

Best Outdoor Drinking

Aloha Huge sun-drenched terrace overlooking Nieuwe

Maas river, with a focus on sustainability. (p50)

Hotel NY Terrace Bar Watch the action on the water from this sunny spot on the point of Kop van Zuid. (p93)

Biergarten Beer, barbecue and a student vibe in a popular meeting spot. (pictured; p49)

Suicide Club Fashionable rooftop bar with views over the city rooftops. (p79)

Bokaal The terrace here spills out into Nieuwemarkt and heaves with drinkers on summer nights. (p49)

nhow Bar Sensational view from a balcony terrace in the iconic De Rotterdam building. (p93)

De Ballentent The city's best waterfront pub, with two terraces. (p79)

De Oude Sluis Old-school *bruin café* (pub) overlooking the canal at Delfshaven. (p79)

De Witte Aap The most popular bar on Witte de Withstraat, with plenty of streetside tables. (p50)

Best Clubs

Maassilo The city's largest club, with gritty surrounds and a powerful sound system. (p93)

Toffler Techno temple set in an old pedestrian tunnel. (p51)

Noah Tiki cocktails, and funk, soul and R&B on the turntable. (p51)

Suicide Club Weekend-only dance floor attracting the bold and the beautiful. (p79)

Architecture

Rotterdam is a vast open-air museum of modern and contemporary architecture. There are many triumphs, including some marvellous buildings by architecture firms OMA and MVRDV, as well as a fair number of magnificent failures. One thing that they all have in common is a willingness to innovate and experiment with built form.

Post-War Reconstruction

The devastating German bombardment and subsequent firestorm that Rotterdam suffered in May 1940 levelled the city's medieval centre and destroyed many other city neighbourhoods. At the war's end, authorities were quick to begin a massive rebuilding program and did so in a visionary way, determining to build a modern city that looked to the future rather than one that emulated the city of the past. An exhilarating building boom ensued and continued for decades, characterised by innovative urban design and cutting-edge architecture. As well as local architects, luminaries including Marcel Breuer, Renzo Piano and Wim Quist have designed city buildings here over the decades.

Rem Koolhaas

Although many well-known architects are based in Rotterdam, one in particular has become synonymous with the city. Rem Koolhaas and his firm The Office of Metropolitan Architecture (OMA) have designed some of Rotterdam's most distinctive buildings and have made a major contribution to the development of its reputation as one of the world's most exciting architectural landscapes. OMA's works include Kunsthal (p40), De Rotterdam (p88) and Timmerhuis (pictured; p45). Upcoming projects include a new stadium for the Feyenoord football club.

FRANS BLOK/SHUTTERSTOCK ©

Best Contemporary Buildings

Centraal Station The most used – and quite possibly best loved – building in Rotterdam. (p143)

Markthal Extraordinary inverted-U-shaped market hall designed by local architecture firm MVRDV. (p40)

De Rotterdam A 'vertical city' designed by Pritzker-winning local hero Rem Koolhaas. (p88)

Timmerhuis Koolhaas' 'floating cloud' constructed from steel and glass. (p45)

Best Modernist Buildings

Van Nelle Fabriek World Heritage–listed icon of 20th-century industrial architecture. (p66)

Huis Sonneveld Dutch Functionalist house dating from 1933. (p34)

Het Industriegebouw One of Rotterdam's many notable office buildings from the post-war reconstruction. (p45)

Best City Symbols

Erasmusbrug This graceful pylon bridge spans the Maas river. (p89)

Overblaak Development Piet Blom's vibrantly coloured, crazily tilting apartment block is as zany as it is memorable. (p43)

Building Nicknames

Many of Rotterdam's buildings have nicknames. Regularly used examples are 'The Swan' (Erasmusbrug) and 'The Pencil' for the apartment tower in the Overblaak Development.

Art

An appreciation of art is something that seems to be built into the DNA of Rotterdammers, and their city is replete with galleries, museums and street sculptures, with countless artworks to be appreciated in buildings, parks and streets.

Museumpark

Located on the western edge of Centrum, the Museumpark is home to Rotterdam's major cultural institutions. Laid out in 1927, the park features trees, lawns, water features and public sculptures and is a popular meeting and relaxation spot for locals. Around its edge are art-filled museums and galleries including the Kunsthal (pictured; p40), Het Nieuwe Instituut (p42) and Museum Boijmans van Beuningen – the latter is closed for renovations (p18). In August, the park hosts Pleinbioscoop Rotterdam (p53), the biggest outdoor cinema in Europe.

Art Street

Contemporary art has a high profile in the city, and is best viewed at one of the contemporary cultural institutions on Witte de Withstraat. Collectively known as the Kunstblock Rotterdam (Arts Block Rotterdam; http://kunstblock.nl), the institutions here include the Witte de With Centre for Contemporary Art (p40), TENT (p41) and Showroom Mama (p42). Try to catch Art Evening, held every Friday, when the venues are free to visit from 6pm to 9pm.

Street Sculpture

Rotterdam's not just an open-air gallery of extraordinary architecture – it's also home to streets filled with art. Well over 60 sculptures are scattered throughout town – with more appearing every year – including many by

ANA DEL CASTILLO/SHUTTERSTOCK ©

major artists. For a full list of sculptures and an interactive map of their locations, visit Sculpture International Rotterdam (www. sculptureinternationalrotterdam.nl) or Visual Arts & Public Space Rotterdam (http://www.bkor.nl/plattegrond/).

Best Art Museums and Galleries

Kunsthal Dynamic cultural institution hosting a constantly changing and consistently excellent exhibition program. (p40)

Witte de With Centre for Contemporary Art Presents experimental exhibitions, installations and events. (p40)

Nederlands Fotomuseum This showcase of Dutch photography also hosts travelling exhibitions of the work of big-name photographers from around the world. (p88)

Showroom Mama One of the main proponents of youth culture in the city, programming plenty of exhibitions and events. (p42)

TENT Stages exhibitions focussing on the work of local contemporary artists. (p41)

Museums

They may be modest in size and relatively few in number, but Rotterdam's museums are as diverse as they are engaging. A number are clustered in the Museumpark precinct and can be visited in one day.

BRIAN S/SHUTTERSTOCK ©

Rotterdam Welcome Card

This discount card (p145) gives discounts on many of Rotterdam's museums, including most museums mentioned on this page.

Best History Museums

Museum Rotterdam
Profiles the city's past and present, and predicts the future. (p40)

Museum Rotterdam '40-'45 NU A multimedia presentation and plenty of artefacts tell the story of Rotterdam during WWII. (p68)

Verhalenhuis Kaap Belvédère Personal stories of individuals and communities living in the city. (p89)

Best Design Museums

Het Nieuwe Instituut
Thought-provoking exhibitions on architecture, design and digital culture, plus a design archive. (pictured; p42)

Huis Sonneveld House museum that can be explored on a fascinating audiotour. (p34)

Nederlands Fotomuseum
A showcase of local and international photography. (p88)

Museum Boijmans van Beuningen Closure

Rotterdam's main museum – Boijmans van Beuningen, in Museumpark – is one of the country's great cultural institutions. From early 2019 it will be closed for major renovations, expected to take seven years.

Tours

The Rotterdam tourist office (p147) on Coolsingel can organise private guides specialising in everything from photography to food, shopping and cycling. Two companies – De Rotterdam Tours and Urban Guides – specialise in architecture tours.

MARIOGUTI/GETTY IMAGES ©

De Rotterdam Tours (www.derotterdamtours. nl) Led by experts, these tours are a great choice for architecture buffs. Offerings include a one-hour tour of Markthal and the Overblaak cube houses (€15.95); a 2½-hour 'Tour of Titans' visiting De Rotterdam building, Markthal and cube houses (€29.95); and a 2½-hour 'Turbo Tour', visiting De Rotterdam, Centraal Station, Timmerhuis and Markthal (€29.95).

Urban Guides (☏010-433 22 31; www.urban guides.nl; Schiekade 205; boat tour adult/child under 12 €17/free; ⏰office 10am-6pm Mon-Sat,

noon-5pm Sun; Ⓜ Stadhuis, 🚊 Pompenburg, Weena, Stadhuis) This group of passionate Rotterdammers offers a selection of architecture-focused outings, including a one-hour boat tour on weekends at 3pm (May to October only).

Line 10 (www.lijn10. nl; adult/child 4-11 €9/7; ⏰departures 11am-4.30pm Tue-Sun Jul-Aug, Thu-Sun Apr-Jun & Sep-Oct) Ride a historic tram through the city on Line 10 (pictured), which stops at 14 destinations around town. Tickets are valid all day, so you can hop on and off as you like. Buy tickets on board (cash or card).

S'dam Gin Tour (www. sdam.nl/zien-doen/ tours-tickets/info/gin-tour-sdam_1; €34.95; ⏰2.30-5pm Sat) This 2.5km guided walking tour of Schiedam's historic distillers' district visits the *waag* (weighing house) and other buildings associated with the *jenever* (Dutch gin) industry. It includes a stop at the National Jenevermuseum Schiedam, where various Schiedam gins are tasted. Reach Schiedam (west of Rotterdam) by watertaxi, train, metro or tram.

Entertainment

Music dominates the city's entertainment programs, with plenty of festivals and venues on offer. Many live-music venues resist being confined to one genre, programming everything from jazz to rock, reggae to R&B.

DIMITRI HAKKE/REDFERNS VIA GETTY IMAGES ©

Best Jazz Clubs

Bird Jazz Club Rotterdam's main jazz venue, with an impressive line-up of musicians. (p63)

Dizzy Decades-old jazz cafe with live music most nights. (p80)

Café LaBru Laid-back bar with live Wednesday-night gigs. (p50)

Best Live-Music Venues

Annabel Mid-size venue hosting musical acts in every genre. (p51)

Rotown Big-name and emerging bands take to the stage here in this bar/music venue/restaurant. (pictured: Matt Flegel on stage; p80)

De Doelen Prestigious venue hosting classical, jazz and world music concerts. (p52)

Worm Caters to fans of experimental and avant-garde music. (p51)

North Sea Jazz Festival

The city's jazz clubs host plenty of after-parties during Rotterdam's world-famous **jazz festival** (p21) in July, and everyone is welcome. There are also plenty of free street performances at this time.

Festivals & Events

The city's program of festivals and events is deliciously diverse. Taking pride of place in the annual festival line-up is North Sea Jazz Festival, which attracts performers and aficionados from around the globe. More local in flavour but just as beloved is Rotterdam Unlimited, a celebration of the city's cultural diversity.

BAS RABELING/SHUTTERSTOCK ©

Rotterdam Architecture Month (http://rotterdamarchitecturemonth.com/; ☾Jun) Established in 2018, this annual festival offers guided architecture walking and cycling tours (some in English), site visits, exhibitions and workshops.

Metropolis Festival (www.metropolisfestival.nl; admission free; ☾early Jul; Ⓜ Zuidplein) One of the largest events held in the city, this one-day festival held in Zuiderpark features up-and-coming bands from around the world. Crowds can number more than 35,000.

North Sea Jazz Festival (www.northseajazz.nl; ☾mid-Jul) One of the world's most-respected jazz events sees hundreds of musicians perform. A free 'North Sea Round Town' festival in the weeks preceding the festival proper sees a variety of jazz acts performing in public spaces and concert halls around the city.

Rotterdam Unlimited (Rotterdam Unlimited; www.zomercarnaval.nl; ☾last weekend in Jul) Rotterdam's multicultural make-up is a vital part of its lifeblood, with some 170 nationalities calling it home. A cacophonous 'battle of drums' and colourful street parade (pictured) are highlights of this vibrant annual celebration, but there are plenty of other outdoor events to enjoy.

Rotterdam Pride (https://rotterdam-pride.com/en/; ☾late Sep) This three-day LGBTI festival includes a Pride walk, parties, seminars and other events.

Shopping

Shopping isn't a major preoccupation here, but those visitors seeking to indulge in a spot of retail therapy will be successful in their quest if they head to the Centrum or Noord neighbourhoods. Locally designed products (particularly homewares and fashion accessories) are worth seeking out.

HEMIS/ALAMY STOCK PHOTO ©

Markets

Every day is market day in Rotterdam, and people are particularly supportive of local artisan producers and craftspeople. Markthal (p40) and Fenix Food Factory (p90) are open daily, and the eco-conscious De Groene Passage (p52), a hybrid market and shopping centre, is open most days of the week. The Blaak (aka Binnenrotte) Street Market next to the Markthal is held on Tuesdays and Saturdays and is the largest street market in the city.

Best Shopping

Groos Stylish concept store selling designer items made in Rotterdam. (pictured; p52)

De Groene Passage Specialises in eco-conscious and sustainable products. (p52)

Rotterdam Tourist Information Gift Shop Books, cards and classy souvenirs. (p147)

Donner The city's best bookstore, with a good selection of English-language books. (p53)

Fenix Food Factory Fabulously fresh artisan produce. (p90)

Whiskybase Massive collection of whiskies, with its own whisky festival. (p63)

Petra Jongmans Artisan-made silver jewellery. (p81)

Rotterdam Vintage Trail

Dapper dressers of both sexes will enjoy browsing the city's vintage boutiques when in town. For a handy vintage shopping guide, go to www.vintagerouterotterdam.com.

Activities

The major activity here is cycling and there's an extensive network of bike paths, including a 28km route along the north and south banks of the Nieuwe Maas. Taking a boat tour is a popular activity in the warmer months, as is taking a bicycle on the Waterbus to Kinderdijk, where it's possible to cycle along the windmill-lined canals.

IRIS VAN DEN BROEK/SHUTTERSTOCK ©

Rebus (☎06 55 82 64 63; www.rebus-info.nl; adult/ child under 12 €17.50/12.50; ⊘noon Tue-Sun Apr-Oct; MLeuvehaven) Four-hour boat tours from Rotterdam that allow a fairly quick visit to Kinderdijk.

Spido (www.spido.nl; Willemsplein 85; adult/ child €13.25/8; ⊘hrs vary; MLeuvehaven, 🚊Leuvehaven, Willemsplein) Harbour tours (pictured) lasting 75 minutes depart from the pier at Leuvehoofd near the Erasmusbrug. There are up

to 10 departures daily in July and August, fewer during the rest of the year.

Waterbus (www.waterbus. nl; Willemskade) Fast-ferry service linking Rotterdam with Dordrecht (line 20) all year, and Rotterdam to Dordrecht via Kinderdijk (line 202) between May and October. Boats leave from Erasmusbrug. There are also services to the historic town of Schiedam immediately west of the city.

Whisper Boat (www. sdam.nl/rondvaarten/ info/vertrek-tijden; Lange Haven 99, Schiedam; adult/ child 4-12 €6.50/3.50; ⊘11.45am, 1.30pm & 3pm Tue-Sun mid-Apr–mid-Oct; MSchiedam Centrum or Parkweg) Take a *fluisterboot* (whisper boat) tour along the canals in Schiedam, west of central Rotterdam, passing historic warehouses, distilleries and windmills en route.

Cycling Routes

Popular cycling routes include the 10km **Roaming Rotterdam**, 15km **Rondje Katendrecht** and 28km **Nieuwe Maasparcours**. The tourist office (p147) on Coolsingel can provide maps and further information.

For Free

The most enjoyable activity in Rotterdam – and the one that draws a constant stream of visitors from around the globe – is wandering the city's streets and admiring its extraordinary architecture and urban design. Needless to say, no fees apply when doing this, or when exploring most building interiors.

ZIVKO TRIKIC/SHUTTERSTOCK ©

Best Parks & Gardens

Het Park Join the locals exercising and relaxing in the city's best-loved park. (p74)

Kralingse Bos & Plas Bucolic park with a lake, forest and windmills; great to explore by bike. (p59)

Tuin Schoonoord Bijou 19th-century landscaped garden perfect for quiet contemplation. (p45)

Best Free Museums & Galleries

Het Nieuwe Instituut Entry to the city's design-driven cultural hub is free on Thursday nights. (p42)

Maritiem Museum Rotterdam The museum itself requires paid entry, but you can wander past its collection of historic vessels (pictured) in Leuvehaven harbour without a ticket. (p42)

Museum Rotterdam Entry to the city museum is free on the first Saturday of every month. (p40)

Showroom Mama Free art exhibitions, performances and events. (p42)

Witte de With Centre for Contemporary Art Contemplate cutting-edge art for free on Friday evenings. (p40)

TENT Another Witte de Withstraat gallery that offers free entry on Friday evenings. (p41)

Toko 51 Free pop-up exhibitions and music gigs. (p75)

Rotterdam Discovery

The Tourist Office (p147) on Coolsingel is home to the free 'Rotterdam Discovery' exhibit, which offers plenty of fascinating information about the city's history, architecture and culture.

For Kids

Rotterdam offers plenty of activities for families travelling with children. There are parks for little ones to play in, loads of museums with kid-friendly activities and an exciting array of boats and trams to board. If bribery is needed to ensure good behaviour, the city's array of artisan ice cream parlours will assist.

KIM KAMINSKI/ALAMY STOCK PHOTO ©

Best Kid-Friendly Museums

Maritiem Museum Rotterdam Older children love the interactive 'Offshore Experience' exhibition; little ones prefer to visit 'Professor Splash'. (p42)

Natural History Museum Delivering facts about the natural world in a fun way. (p42)

Wereldmuseum Celebrates the city's multicultural heritage, with a dedicated children's section. (p43)

Best Family-Friendly Eating

Parqiet Parents can enjoy an excellent coffee while kids play on the lawn of this cute cafe in Het Park. (p77)

By Jarmusch Teenagers will adore this 1950s-style American diner. (pictured; p48)

De IJsmaker The city's best ice cream, with several stores across the city. (p46)

Tante Nel The best French fries in town. (p46)

Angelo Betti Top-notch pizza and gelato. Need we say more? (p60)

Urban Bakery Colourful cupcakes and fabulously rich fudge to eat in or take away. (p61)

Supermercado Tacos and empanadas. Messy but fun. (p49)

Saving with Kids

○ Some museums offer free entry for children under 18.

○ Discounted transport rates for children usually apply.

Four Perfect Days

Day 1

Start your day at architecturally splendiferous **Centraal Station** (p143), walk down Lijnbaan shopping street and then visit **Museum Rotterdam** (p40) to learn about the city's history and culture. Enjoy lunch at **Pierre** (p45) or **AJÍ** (p45) in the fashionable Meent district, pop into **Markthal** (p40) and then take a watertaxi to Kop van Zuid to admire its cutting-edge architecture. Admire the view over the Nieuwe Maas river while enjoying a drink at the **Hotel NY Terrace Bar** (p93), then cross the Rijnhaven pedestrian bridge to visit the **Fenix Food Factory** (pictured; p90) before spending the night in Deliplein (p92), a popular eating and entertainment precinct.

Day 2

IRIS VAN DEN BROEK/SHUTTERSTOCK ©

Devote the morning to the ever-changing exhibitions at **Kunsthal** (p40). Enjoy lunch and coffee at **Hopper** (p47). Next, visit **Huis Sonneveld** (p34), a wonderful example of 1930s Dutch Functionalist architecture. Afterwards, take a tram to historic **Delfshaven** (pictured; p70), one of the few neighbourhoods in Rotterdam to emerge unscathed from the WWII bombings. Wander around the canal, pausing to enjoy one of the house brews at **Stadsbrouwerij De Pelgrim** (p79). Head back to Centrum to spend the night eating and drinking on everyone's favourite party strip, **Witte de Withstraat**.

Day 3

Kick-start your day with a coffee at **Urban Espresso Bar** (p75) before checking out the exhibitions at the **Kunsthal** (p40). Then take a leisurely walk through leafy **Het Park** (pictured; p74). For lunch, claim a deckchair on the lawn at **Parqiet** (p77), a cafe in the park's old coach house. In the afternoon, visit the **Maritiem Museum Rotterdam** (p42) and then join the after-work crowd for a cocktail at sophisticated **Stirr** (p50) or a beer at down-to-earth **Biergarten** (p49). Have dinner at one of the neighbourhood bistros in Noord, then head to **Bird Jazz Club** (p63) to while the night away listening to world-class jazz acts.

Day 4

BJOERN WYLEZICH/SHUTTERSTOCK ©

Climb aboard a Waterbus (pictured) to **Kinderdijk** (p136), a postcard-perfect Dutch landscape of canals, marshes and windmills 19km southeast of Rotterdam. Hire a bike from the souvenir shop at the site and peddle your way along the Kinderdijk Cycle Route. Alternatively, saunter along the pedestrian-friendly path between the site's two canals, stopping to watch the windmill sails slowly turning in the breeze. Your visit finished, take a Waterbus back to Rotterdam and dine on ultrafresh seafood at **Zeezout** (p47). Then spend your last night in town at the **Suicide Club** (p79), an edgy rooftop bar where you can dance and drink the night away.

Need to Know

For detailed information, see Survival Guide p141

Currency
Euro (€)

Languages Spoken
Dutch; many people
also speak English

Money
ATMs are widely
available.

Mobile Phones
The Netherlands uses
GSM phones. Local
prepaid SIM cards are
widely available.

Time
Central European Time
(GMT/UTC plus one
hour)

Tipping
Tipping is not
widespread in the
Netherlands.

Visas
Generally not required
for stays of up to
three months. Some
nationalities require a
Schengen visa.

Daily Budget

Budget: Less than €120
Dorm bed: €13–33
A burger or chips dinner: €8–15
Watertaxi ride: €4.50

Midrange: €120–250
Double room: from €100
Evening meal in a bistro: €35
Museum ticket: €17

Top End: More than €250
Luxurious hotel double room: from €180
Dinner in top restaurant with drinks: from €80
Guided architecture tour: €30

Advance Planning

Three months before Book your accommodation – hotels
here fill up fast.

One month before Check the websites of De Rotterdam
Tours (p19) and Urban Guides (p19) to book an architecture
tour.

One week before Check the Agenda section of the Rotterdam Tourist Information (p147) website to find out what
festivals and events are on.

Arriving in Rotterdam

✈ From Schiphol International Airport

Frequent train services (€12.40 to €14.80, 25 to 45 minutes); taxi to Rotterdam's city centre €90.

✈ From Rotterdam The Hague Airport

Bus 33 to Rotterdam Centraal Station (€3.50, 20 minutes); taxi to Rotterdam's city centre €25.

🚉 Rotterdam Centraal

In the city centre; services arrive here from Brussels, Paris and destinations across the Netherlands.

🚌 Bus Interchange

Long-distance buses arrive just west of Centraal Station; there is a Eurolines office in the nearby Groothandelsgebouw building.

Getting Around

🚲 Bike

Extensive grid of bike paths; free bike parking at the huge *fietsenstalling* (bike garage) underneath Centraal Station.

Ⓜ Metro

Excellent system with five lines covering the city and travelling as far as Den Haag.

🚊 Tram

An efficient network covering most of the city; major interchanges at Centraal Station and Beurs.

⛴ Ferry

Fast watertaxis ply the Nieuwe Maas. Tickets are charged by distance travelled.

🚗 Car & Motorcycle

Paid parking garages and street parks across the city.

Rotterdam Neighbourhoods

Noord (p55)
Gradually gentrifying, this multicultural district is gaining a reputation for its cafe culture, microbreweries and offbeat boutiques.

Centrum (p33)
The geographic heart of the city, Centrum is home to iconic buildings, big-hitting cultural institutions and a diverse array of restaurants, cafes, bars and shops.

Van Nelle Fabriek

Huis Sonneveld

Museum Rotterdam '40-'45 NU

West (p65)
The pace is slow and the neighbourhood feel is pronounced in the suburbs west of the city centre, which include the areas that escaped destruction during WWII.

Zuid (p83)
The districts south of the river are characterised by their innovative urban design, cutting-edge modern architecture and popular eating and entertainment venues.

Explore Rotterdam

Life moves at a fast pace in the Netherlands' second city. Locals joke that the city slogan should be 'no talk, just action', and there sure is plenty of the latter. With the country's largest multicultural population, a fast-growing tourism sector and an ongoing building boom, this is a city that adapts to change and challenge with real panache.

Explore

Centrum

When exploring Centrum you'll probably spend more time looking up than ahead, visually sidetracked by its profusion of visually arresting high-rise buildings. Many of these date from the 1940s and 1950s, but some are new – and extremely exciting – arrivals. Indoors, there are plenty of museums and galleries to visit.

This neighbourhood is compact and easy to navigate. Start your exploration at Centraal Station (p41), then head south towards the waterfront, branching off the main axis, Mauritsweg, to visit the cultural institutions around Museumpark (p16). Next, explore the streets and sites in the Cool District. Don't miss Markthal (p40) and the fashionable streets around Meent, where you can stop for lunch. Then to Witte de Withstraat, Rotterdam's party and arts street, where you can gallery-hop, eat, drink and dance the rest of the day away.

Getting There & Around

🚃 You can transfer from intercity trains to metro and trams at both Centraal and Blaak stations.

Ⓜ Stations are Rotterdam Centraal, Blaak, Beurs, Leuve-haven, Eendrachtsplein and Stadhuis.

🚌 Major stops include Centraal Station, Blaak, Stadhuis and Museumpark.

⛴ Watertaxi docks include Boompjes, Leuvehaven/Main-port Hotel and Willemskade/Waterbus.

Neighbourhood Map on p38

Markthal (p40) VICTOR MASCHEK/SHUTTERSTOCK ©

Top Sights 📷
Huis Sonneveld

Replete with original fittings and furniture, the Sonneveld House transports visitors back to 1930s Rotterdam, when local architects were embracing Functionalism and designing streamlined and resolutely modern buildings for their clients to work and live in. This aesthetically pared-back but technology-rich house is one of the greatest examples of this significant architectural movement.

◉ MAP P38, A4

www.huissonneveld.nl

Jongkindstraat 25

adult/student/child under 18 €10/6.50/free

🕙 10am-5pm Tue-Sat

Ⓜ Eendrachtsplein,
🚋 Museumpark

The Architecture

When wealthy businessman Albertus Sonneveld decided to commission an architect to design a contemporary home for his family, the obvious choice was Leendert van der Vlugt, who had designed the magnificent Van Nelle Factory (p66) where Sonneveld was a company director. Working with Johannes Brinkman, Van der Vlugt designed a streamlined, state-of-the-art building that was hailed as an outstanding example of Dutch Functionalism as soon as its construction was completed in 1933.

Life for the Sonnevelds

The complimentary multilanguage audiotour makes a visit here particularly worthwhile. On your self-guided tour, you'll hear about the history of the building and its occupants, and learn plenty of facts about the custom-designed furniture, state-of-the-art appliances and advanced building techniques utilised in the house. Walking through the house – which is full of light, courtesy of banks of windows and a number of balconies – it is easy to imagine what daily life must have been like for the Sonneveld family and their servants.

Distinctive Features

It's clear from the minute you enter that this house must have been unusual when it was built. Its colour scheme would have been considered daringly modern at the time – especially the turquoise blue tiles in the bathrooms. Modern technologies are well represented (Mrs Sonneveld was particularly keen on labour-saving devices) and the floors are covered in linoleum, a new and expensive product at the time. You'll be able to marvel at these and other distinctive features on your visit.

★ **Top Tips**

o Be sure to use the free audiotour that is offered with your entrance ticket.

o When using the audiotour, listen to the background narratives that are contained within it. These provide information about the design, construction and furnishing of the house; and also describe the daily lives of its residents.

o Take advantage of the free entrance to nearby Het Nieuwe Instituut (p42) that is included in your entrance ticket.

✗ **Take a Break**

The bookshop cafe on the ground floor of Het Nieuwe Instituut (p42) has stylish surrounds, a casual vibe and a simple menu.

The popular cafes, bars and restaurants on Witte de Withstaat and Schiedamse Vest are a short walk away – Hopper (p47) is one of our favourites.

Walking Tour 🥾

Meent & Around

The neighbourhood southeast of Meent in the city centre is one of the most vibrant in Rotterdam, with boutiques, bars and eateries aplenty. This is a part of town where workers and students catch up with friends at the end of the day, where families and couples come to dine out and where shoppers busily browse boutiques and markets.

Walk Facts

Start De Groene Passage
End Tante Nel
Length 1.9km; 90 minutes

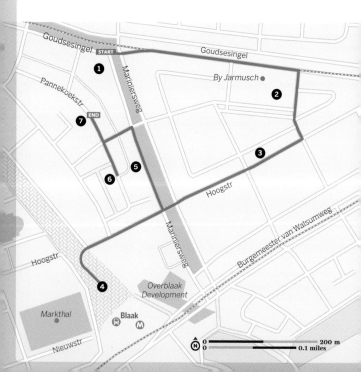

❶ De Groene Passage

One of Rotterdam's hip indoor markets, this emporium (p52) hosts stalls selling eco-conscious and sustainable goods including food, soaps, clothing, homewares, furniture and textiles. On Saturdays, organic food stalls sometimes set up on the street outside.

❷ Het Industriegebouw

Home to architectural studios, coworking spaces, design boutiques and an array of eateries, the recently restored and reimagined 1950s Het Industriegebouw (p45) was designed by architect Hugh Maaskant in collaboration with Willem van Tijen. It's now home to popular cafes including quirky By Jarmusch (p48), a 1950s-style American diner.

❸ Verward

Wine is the emphasis at this ultrawelcoming neighbourhood bar (p49), where owner/sommelier Ward de Zeeuw pours from a constantly changing selection of bottles to keep his many regulars happy. The small but tasty food menu means that many customers settle in for a long session.

❹ Blaak Markt

One of the largest street markets in the Netherlands, Blaak Markt (p53) takes over the square east of the Markthal on Tuesdays and Saturdays. After visiting, you should also visit Markthal (p40) – consider signing up in advance for a guided visit covering the building's architectural and foodie highlights; book via info@markthal.nl.

❺ Balanz-s

Rotterdammers are an active lot, and if they're not cycling their way around the city they can often be found in yoga and pilates studios like **Balanz-s** (☏ 010-307 27 59; www.balanzs.nl/studio/rotterdam-mariniersweg/; Mariniersweg 151; ☉ hrs vary; Ⓜ Blaak, 🚊 Blaak) on Mariniersweg. Drop in to join locals enjoying Hatha, Vinyasa, Bikram and other sessions.

❻ Bokaal

An oldie but a goodie, Bokaal (p49) is one of the city's best-known bars and a popular neighbourhood meeting place. In good weather, the terrace is a perfect people-watching spot.

❼ Tante Nel

After drinking at Bokaal, it's almost obligatory to adjourn to this much-loved chips stand (p46), where the order of choice is *patat stoofvlees* (fries topped with a rich meat stew) – fantastically warming in winter but delicious in every season.

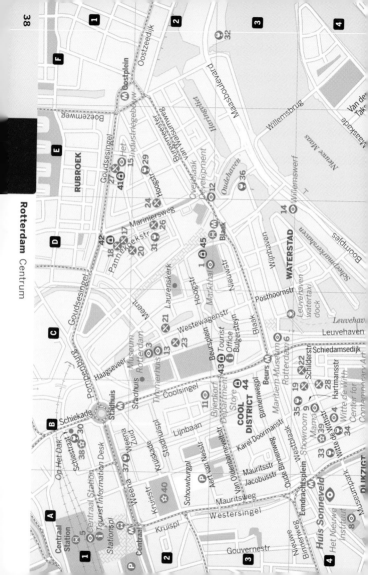

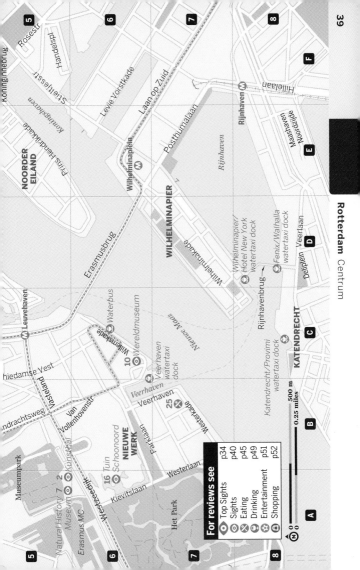

Rosestr

Koninginnebrug

Haringpldsplein

Steltjesstr

Prins Hendrikkade

Koningshaven

Levie Vorstkade

Laan op Zuid

Wilhelminaplein

Posthumalaan

NOORDER EILAND

WILHELMINAPIER

Rijnhaven

Hillelaan

Rijnhaven

Maashaven Noordzijde

Erasmusbrug

Wilhelminakade

Wilhelminapier/
Hotel New York
watertaxi dock

Fenix/Walhalla
watertaxi dock

Delfplein

Veerlaan

Rijnhavenbrug

KATENDRECHT

Leuvehaven

Waterbus

Willemskade

Wereldmuseum

Nieuwe Maas

Veerhaven
watertaxi
dock

Katendrecht/Provimi
watertaxi dock

hiedamse Vest

Vasteland

Van Vollenhovenstr

Veerhaven

Veerhaven

Weerkade

ndrachtsweg

Museumpark

Natural History 7 2
Museum MC

Kingstr

Tuin

Schoonoord

NIEUWE WERK

Parklaan

Westerlaan

Erasmus MC

Westzeedijk

Kievitslaan

Het Park

For reviews see

◉	Top Sights	p34
◉	Sights	p40
⊗	Eating	p45
◉	Drinking	p49
◉	Entertainment	p51
◉	Shopping	p52

500 m

0.25 miles

A B C D E F

5 6 7 8

Sights

Markthal
NOTABLE BUILDING

1 ⊙ MAP P38, D2

One of the city's signature buildings, this extraordinary inverted-U-shaped market hall was designed by local architecture firm MVRDV and opened for business in 2014. It comprises highly sought-after glass-walled apartments arcing over a 40m-high market hall with a striking fruit-and-vegetable-muralled ceiling. Most of the stalls sell food to eat on the spot rather than produce to take home. There are also a number of sit-down eateries. (Market Hall; https://markthal.klepierre.nl/; Nieuwstraat; ⊙10am-8pm Mon-Thu & Sat, to 9pm Fri, noon-6pm Sun; Ⓜ Blaak, 🚆 Blaak)

Kunsthal
GALLERY

2 ⊙ MAP P38, A5

This dynamic cultural institution in Rotterdam's main museum enclave is known for its constantly changing and inevitably thought-provoking exhibition program. There are always at least three exhibitions to visit – from painting to photography, fashion to graphic design – and these are spread across the architecturally notable multifloored building, which abuts a dyke embankment and was designed in 1988–89 by Rem Koolhaas and Fuminori Hoshino from local firm OMA. (📞010-440 03 00; www.kunsthal.nl; Westzeedijk 341; adult/student/child €14/7/free; ⊙10am-5pm Tue-Sat, 11am-5pm Sun; 🚆Kievitslaan)

Museum Rotterdam
MUSEUM

3 ⊙ MAP P38, C2

The attractive Timmerhuis (p45) building designed by Rotterdam-based Rem Koolhaas is a classy location for this museum profiling the city's past, present and future. There are three main exhibits – an engaging 'History of the City' exhibit on the ground floor with plenty of artefacts and scale models of the city in 1694, 1940 and now; a multimedia space focusing on the stories of local residents; and an upstairs space for temporary exhibitions – as well as a small kids' play area. (📞010-217 67 50; www.museumrotterdam.nl; Rodezand 26; adult/student/child 4-17 €7.50/3.75/2.50, free 1st Sat of the month; ⊙10am-5pm Tue-Sat, 11am-5pm Sun; Ⓜ Stadhuis, 🚆Stadhuis)

Witte de With Center for Contemporary Art
MUSEUM

4 ⊙ MAP P38, B4

Sharing a premises with TENT (p41), this gallery has its finger on the pulse of breaking developments in contemporary art worldwide. Its experimental exhibitions, installations and events have a laser-sharp social and political focus, and often launch up-and-coming talent. It closes between exhibitions while new works are being set up, so check ahead to make sure it's open. In 2018, the

The Great Kunsthal Heist

In 2012, Rotterdam's Kunsthal (p40) hit the headlines for all the wrong reasons. In the early hours of an October morning, thieves broke into the museum and stole seven paintings: two by Monet, and one each by Picasso, Gaugin, Matisse, Freud and De Haan. Together, they were valued somewhere between €50 million and €100 million.

The following year, art lovers the world over were horrified to learn that the paintings were thought to have been destroyed in Romania by the mother of Radu Dogaru, one of the thieves, after he was arrested for the crime. Remnants of paint, canvas and nails were found in an oven in which she is said to have incinerated them. Dogaru and another Romanian subsequently confessed to the crime and were sentenced to lengthy jail terms. Dogaru's mother Olga was convicted of transporting and hiding stolen property, and sentenced to a two-year jail term.

After the heist, the gallery underwent an extensive renovation and a (clearly much needed) security upgrade.

gallery announced that it was considering a name change, but no final decision had been made at the time of writing. (📞010-411 01 44; www.wdw.nl; Witte de Withstraat 50; adult/student & child under 18 €6/3, free entry Fri 6-9pm, combination ticket with TENT €9/4.50; ⏱11am-6pm Tue-Thu, Sat & Sun, to 9pm Fri; Ⓜ Eendrachtsplein, 🚊Museumpark)

TENT GALLERY

On the ground floor of the Witte de With Center for Contemporary Art (p40), this gallery (see 4 ◉ Map p38, B4) stages equally impressive contemporary art shows but differs in that it focuses on work by local artists. (📞010-411 01 44; www.tentrotterdam.nl; Witte de Withstraat 50; adult/student & child under 18

€5/2.50, free entry Fri 6-9pm, combination ticket with Witte de With Center €9/4.50; ⏱11am-6pm Tue-Thu, Sat & Sun, to 9pm Fri; Ⓜ Eendrachtsplein, 🚊Museumpark)

Centraal Station ARCHITECTURE

5 ◉ MAP P38, A1

Rotterdam's main transport hub, the latest incarnation of busy Centraal Station was designed by Benthem Crouwel, MVSA and West 8. Built between 1999 and 2013, it features a dramatically angled passenger hall with a pointed, stainless-steel clad roof that almost punches into the sky. (www.ns.nl/stationsinformatie/rtd/rotterdam-centraal; Stationsplein 1; Ⓜ Rotterdam Centraal, 🚊Centraal)

Maritiem Museum Rotterdam

MUSEUM

6 ◉ MAP P38, C3

Children adore this museum overlooking Leuvehaven, whose permanent exhibits are emphatically kid-focused. The best of these is the 'Offshore Experience', which investigates day-to-day operations on North Sea oil and gas platforms and includes nine interactive activities. Older kids can test their dexterity with crane simulators, take safety quizzes, steer ships with a joystick and more. Little ones will get more out of the 'Professor Splash' play activity. Adults can engage with temporary exhibitions, which deal with all things maritime. (Maritime Museum; 📞 010-413 26 80; www.maritiemmuseum.nl; Leuvehaven 1; adult/student & child over 4 €12.50/9; ⏱10am-5pm Tue-Sat, 11am-5pm Sun; 🚻; Ⓜ Beurs, 🚊 Beurs)

Natural History Museum

MUSEUM

7 ◉ MAP P38, A5

Geared predominantly towards children, the collection at this small museum focuses on delivering facts in a fun way. The 'Uitslovers' ('Show-offs') exhibit profiles the biggest, most unique and most unusual animals, while the 'Biodiversity' exhibit delivers loads of information about animal and plant species. There are also plenty of bones and fossils to look at, including the assembled skeleton of a huge Asian elephant called Ramon. (Het Natuurhistorisch; 📞 010-436 42 22; www.hetnatuurhistorisch.nl; Westzeedijk 345; adult/student & child 5-15 €7/3.50; ⏱11am-5pm Tue-Sun; 🚻; 🚊 Kievitslaan)

Het Nieuwe Instituut

MUSEUM

8 ◉ MAP P38, A4

This design-driven cultural hub houses the Netherlands Architecture Institute, e-culture institute Virtueel Platform and the Netherlands Institute for Design and Fashion. Architect Jo Coenen beat high-profile competitors including Rem Koolhaas to win the 1988 design competition for the building: a striking glass, concrete and steel structure incorporating multiple exhibition spaces, an archive and an auditorium overlooking a lake. Its exhibitions on architecture, design and digital culture can be esoteric and are geared towards design professionals rather than the general public. (📞 010-440 12 00; www.hetnieuweinstituut.nl; Museumpark 25; adult/student/child €14/7/free; ⏱11am-5pm Tue, Wed & Fri-Sun, to 9pm Thu; Ⓜ Eendrachtsplein, 🚊 Museumpark)

Showroom Mama

ARTS CENTRE

9 ◉ MAP P38, B4

One of the main proponents of youth culture in Rotterdam, Showroom Mama hosts art exhibitions, performances, events and installations by aspiring creatives. (📞 010-233 20 22; www.showroommama.nl; Wiite de Withstraat 29-31;

🕙1-6pm Wed, Thu, Sat & Sun, to 9pm Fri; Ⓜ Beurs, 🚋 Museumpark)

Wereldmuseum

MUSEUM

10 ◉ MAP P38, C6

Inside the 19th-century Royal Yacht Club building, this ethnographic museum celebrates multiculturalism. Mainly closed for renovation when we last visited, it is scheduled to reopen with a dedicated children's museum in 2019. (World Museum; www.wereldmuseum.nl; Willemskade 25; 🚋 Willemskade)

Bijenkorf Department Store

ARCHITECTURE

11 ◉ MAP P38, B2

Legendary Bauhaus architect Marcel Breuer worked with Amsterdam-based architect Abraham Elzas on the design of this department store, which opened in 1957. The cladding on its Coolsingel facade (distinctive hexagonal travertine panels that look like honeycomb) is a nod to the department store's name: 'Beehive'. It features a monumental sculpture by Russian Constructivisit Naum Gabo on the Coolsingel side. (Coolsingel 105; Ⓜ Beurs, 🚋 Beurs)

Overblaak Development

ARCHITECTURE

12 ◉ MAP P38, E2

Designed by Amsterdam-based architect Piet Blom and built between 1978 and 1984, this mind-bending development facing Markthal is marked by its pencil-shaped tower and 'forest' of 38 cube-shaped apartments on hexagonal pylons.

Bijenkorf department store

Rotterdam: Architecture City

If you're interested in architecture, you'll love Rotterdam. This walkable showpiece of 20th- and 21st-century buildings and innovative urban design is notable as much for its 'city in progress' and 'try anything once' philosophy as it is as a repository for some truly great design.

Dutch Functionalism

Dating from the 1920s, Functionalism was a branch of modernism based on the idea that building design should be based solely on purpose and function, and should create a better world and a better life for the people who lived and worked in them. In Rotterdam, a form of Functionalism came to be known as the Nieuwe Bouwen (New Building). Significant buildings in this style are the Unesco World Heritage–listed Van Nelle Fabriek (p66) and the Huis Sonneveld (p34).

Post-War Reconstruction

After WWII the city was rebuilt. In the port areas, new buildings of note included the Cruise Terminal (p88; 1946–49), designed by Jan Brinkman, Jo van den Broek and Jacob Bakema. In the city centre, notable new buildings included Groothandelsgebouw (1945–52), near Centraal Station, designed by HA Maaskant and W van Tijen.

Reconstruction work continued at a cracking pace during the '50s. Notable additions were the travertine-clad Bijenkorf Department Store (p43), designed by Bauhaus architect Marcel Breuer, opened in 1957; and the De Doelen (p52; 1955–66) concert hall, designed by EHA and HMJH Kraaijvanger and RH Fledderus.

1980s & '90s

Some of the city's signature buildings date from the 1980s and '90s. Chief among these is Piet Blom's 1978–84 Overblaak Development (p43; aka Blaakse Bos or Blaak Forest), with its tilting yellow-and-white cube houses. Other stand-out structures are the Maritime Museum (p42; 1981–86) and the Willemswerf (p45; 1983–89) office tower. Both were designed by Amsterdam-based WG Quist.

Contemporary Masterpieces

The 21st century has seen many great buildings added to the city's skyline. These include Rem Koolhaas' De Rotterdam (p88; 1997–2013) and Timmerhuis (p45; 2009–15); MVRDV's extraordinary Markthal (p40; 2004–14); and Benthem Crouwel, Meyer & Van Schooten's magnificent Centraal Station (p41; 1999–2013).

This vibrantly coloured, crazily tilting apartment block is one of the city's most recognisable structures. One of the cubes can be visited and Stayokay Rotterdam hostel is housed here. (Blaakse Bos; Blaak Woods; www.kubuswoning.nl; Overblaak; Blaak, Blaak)

Timmerhuis ARCHITECTURE

13 MAP P38, C2

Designed by Koolhaas' OMA, the 'Carpenter's House' (2009–15) incorporates apartments, shops, restaurants and Museum Rotterdam (p40). Often described as a 'floating cloud' or the 'cloud house', the building's stepped steel-and-glass cubed mass does indeed seem to float above the street. (Rodezand; Stadhuis, Beurs, Stadhuis, Beurs)

Willemswerf ARCHITECTURE

14 MAP P38, D3

Designed by Dutch architect Wim Quist and completed in 1989, this striking office building has a facade featuring two huge intersecting wedges. (Boompjes 40; Blaak, Blaak)

Het Industriegebouw
ARCHITECTURE

15 MAP P38, E1

Designed by Hugh Maaskant and Willem van Tijen in the post-war reconstruction period and completed in 1952, this building has recently been restored and reopened as a hub for creative industries

and businesses. Tenants include prominent local architecture firm MVRDV. (https://hetindustriegebouw.nl/; Goudsesingel; Kipstraat)

Tuin Schoonoord GARDENS

16 MAP P38, A6

This 1.2-hectare garden dates from the 1860s. It features 1000 or so plant species and has a tranquil pond filled with Japanese carp. (www.tuinschoonoord.nl; Kievitslaan 8; admission free; 8.30am-4.30pm; Kievitslaan)

Eating

AJÍ INTERNATIONAL €€

17 MAP P38, D1

Good-quality Asian food is hard to source in Rotterdam, so we were thrilled to discover this chic bistro serving dishes inspired by Asia and the Mediterranean. Build a meal with a few small plates, or just pop in for drinks and a platter of oysters or Spanish cured meats. There are good wines by the glass and bottle, too. (010-767 01 69; www.restaurantaji.nl; Pannekoekstraat 40a; snacks €5-24, small plates €16-24; noon-2pm & 5-10pm Tue-Thu, noon-11pm Fri & Sat; Meent)

Pierre FRENCH €€

18 MAP P38, D1

Like many locals, we love visiting Pierre at all times of the day. At breakfast, the croissants are buttery; at lunch the baguettes have delectable fillings; and at dinner, classic brasserie dishes (beef bourguignon, duck confit, steak frites) can be ordered as small or large plates. Staff are friendly, street-side tables are sunny and the wine list is excellent. *Formidable!* (📞010-842 37 57; https://pierre.nl/; Pannekoekstraat 38a; mains €8-25; ⏲10am-10pm; 🛜⚕; 🚊Meent)

De IJsmaker ICE CREAM €

19 🗺 MAP P38, B4

Fresh flavours reign supreme at this artisanal ice cream parlour on Witte de Withstraat and only quality produce is used – the simply spectacular pistachio ice cream is made with nuts from Bronte in Sicily and the seductive vanilla is made with beans sourced in Madagascar.

(📞010-341 84 19; http://deijsmaker.nl/ Witte de Withstraat 7a; per scoop €1.30-1.80; ⏲11am-11pm Mon-Sat, from noon Sun; Ⓜ Beurs, 🚊Museumpark)

Tante Nel FAST FOOD €

20 🗺 MAP P38, D2

Differing from traditional *patat* (fries) stands in a number of crucial ways, Tante Nel has street-side seating where its many and varied regulars settle in to enjoy treats such as hand-cut, expertly cooked fries with truffle mayonnaise or *patat stoofvlees* (fries with a rich meat stew), washed down with a gin and tonic, beer or milkshake. (www.tante-nel.com; Pannekoekstraat 53a; fries €2.50-8.75; ⏲noon-10pm Mon-Sat, to 9pm Sun; 🚊Meent)

Dutch Fries: The Lexicon

If you're going to sample Rotterdam's favourite fast food, *friet* or *patat* (Dutch-style French fries), you will need to choose one of the following variations:

Patat met With mayonnaise (the default order)

Patat zonder Plain

Patat met pindasaus With peanut sauce

Patatje joppie With a mixture of mayonnaise, ketchup and spices

Patatje oorlog With peanut sauce, mayonnaise and optional raw chopped onions

Patat curry With curry sauce

Patat stoofvlees With meat stew

Kapsalon With kebab or shawarma and sometimes cheese.

All will come served in a paper cone and are – frankly – best eaten as part of a boozy night on the town.

Dudok

CAFE €€

21 ⊗ MAP P38, C2

Ask any Rotterdammer to nominate their favourite sweet treat, and there's a good chance they will opt for the apple pie served here. A cinnamon-spiced delight, it is best served with a side order of whipped cream. Now a national chain, Dudok opened at this site in 1991 and was named after architect Willem Marinus Dudok, who designed the 1945 former bank building. (☑010-433 31 02; www.dudok.nl; Meent 88; apple pie & cream €4.75; ☻8am-9.30pm Mon-Thu, 8am-10pm Fri, 9am-9.30pm Sat & Sun; Ⓜ Stadhuis)

Hopper

CAFE €

22 ⊗ MAP P38, C4

Roasting its own coffee using single-source beans and offering both espresso and AeroPress styles, this industrial-chic cafe has its own on-site bakery, which makes excellent sourdoughs, pastries and cakes. Enjoy a freshly made sandwich, buttery croissant or hearty soup in the airy dining space or at one of the pavement tables. (www.hopper-coffee.nl; Schiedamse Vest 146; lunch dishes €6-11; ☻8.45am-6pm Mon-Fri, 10am-6pm Sat & Sun; ☏; Ⓜ Beurs, ⊟ Beurs)

Asian Glories

CHINESE €€

23 ⊗ MAP P38, C2

Modern Cantonese, Szechuan and Beijing dishes dominate the menu at this upmarket eatery. Its chefs are good at what they do – the Peking Duck is excellent, and the dumplings and other dim sum dishes are rightfully famous throughout the city – but we wish the menu had a little more depth and variety. Service can be slightly brusque. Bookings advised. (☑010-411 71 07; www.asianglories.nl; Leeuwenstraat 15; dim sum menu €35, set menus €32-82, mains €20-29; ☻noon-10pm Thu-Tue; Ⓜ Stadhuis, Beurs)

O'Pazzo

PIZZA €€

24 ⊗ MAP P38, D2

Generations of Rotterdammers have grown up eating the tasty Neapolitan-style pizzas cooked by Italian *pizzaioli* (pizza makers) in O'Pazzo's huge tiled oven, usually ending their meals with a rich dessert (tiramisu, cheesecake) or bowl of house-made gelato. Service is friendly and efficient, and the Italian house wines are eminently quaffable. Even the coffee is good. Gluten-free pizzas are available. (☑010 282 7107; www. opazzo.nl; Mariniersweg 90; pizzas €11-20, pastas €14-16; ☻5.30-10.30pm Tue & Wed, 11.30am-10.30pm Thu, 11.30am-11pm Fri & Sat, noon-11pm Sun; ☏☑🕭; Ⓜ Blaak)

Zeezout

SEAFOOD €€€

25 ⊗ MAP P38, B7

One of the few restaurants in the city centre to open on Sundays, Zeezout (Sea Salt) is located in the quiet residential Scheepvaartkwartier neighbourhood. Specialising in seafood, it offers a limited number of dishes inspired by global cuisines. (📞010-436 50 49; https://restaurantzeezout.nl/; Westerkade 11; mains €28-30, 3-course lunch menu €35, dinner menus €45-70; 🕐noon-2.30pm & 6-9.30pm Tue-Fri, 12.30-2.30pm & 6-9.30pm Sat, 5.30-8.30pm Sun; 🚊Kievitslaan, Vastelaand)

Picknick

CAFE €

26 🍴 MAP P38, D2

Known for its generous 'Picknick platters', this casual cafe near Markthal has a particularly alluring breakfast menu offering globally inspired dishes such as savoury porridge, coconut ricebread and Moroccan pancakes. The rear courtyard is a lovely spot on a sunny morning. (📞010 223 89 84; www.picknickrotterdam.nl; Mariniersweg 259; breakfast dishes €3.50-12.50, lunch dishes €6-12.50; 🕐8am-4.30pm Mon-Sat, 9am-4.30pm Sun; 📶🖍; 🚇Blaak)

By Jarmusch

DINER €€

27 🍴 MAP P38, E1

If there's one thing that can be said about Rotterdam, it's that it is never predictable. So it's hardly surprising that locals have embraced this thoroughly non-Dutch 1950s American-style diner with open arms. The quality of the eggs, burgers, waffles and subs leaves something to be desired, but the ambience is great – humorous and hip in equal measure. (📞010-307 48 09; www.byjarmusch.nl; Goudsesingel 64; breakfast dishes €6-15, burgers €9-19; 🕐8am-4pm; 🚇Oostplein)

Biergarten

Supermercado

MEXICAN €

28 MAP P38, B4

On Rotterdam's most happening strip, this taqueria serves tacos, ceviche, nachos and empanadas that wouldn't cut the mustard in Mexico but seem to satisfy loads of locals. In summer, the front courtyard with its colourful lights is a lovely spot in which to enjoy a well-priced meal. (☑010-404 80 70; www.supermercadorotterdam.nl; crn Schiedamse Vest & Witte de Withstraat; tacos €3.50, nachos €8; ☺noon-11pm Sun-Thu, to midnight Fri & Sat; Ⓜ Beurs, ⬜ Beurs)

Drinking

Verward

WINE BAR

29 ⬜ MAP P38, E2

Beer is a more common tipple than wine in Rotterdam, so many bars here have less-than-stellar selections of wine by the glass or bottle. That's not the case at this friendly wine bar, where sommelier Ward de Zeeuw pours an interesting selection of Old World wines. Sit at the large wooden bar or outside to enjoy a glass or two. (☑06 5067 0495; www.verward.nl; Hoogstraat 69a; ☺2-11pm Thu-Mon; Ⓜ Blaak, ⬜ Burgemeester van Walsumweg, Kipstraat)

Biergarten

BEER GARDEN

30 ⬜ MAP P38, B1

A sun-bleached labyrinth of wooden tables, brightly painted stairs, exotic foliage and low-slung festoon lighting, the Biergarten

Rooftop Cafe

The 1950s Schieblock office building near Centraal Station is home to one of Rotterdam's most unusual cafes. Perched on top of the building is **Op Het Dak** (Map p38; B1; www.ophetdak.com; Schiekade 189, 7th fl; breakfast dishes €8-13, lunch dishes €8-14; ☺8.30am-5pm Tue-Sat, from 9am Sun; ☑; ⬜ Weena, Pompenburg), a pavilion set amidst one of Europe's largest harvestable rooftop gardens. Its healthy dishes are made using the herbs, vegetables, fruit and honey grown here. In warm weather, tables on the deck or in the garden are popular breakfast and lunch spots.

throngs with thirsty locals enjoying ice-cold pilsner, homemade lemonade and a tempting selection of barbecued meats. On Fridays, DJs preside over the always-inclusive action. (☑010-233 05 56; www.biergartenrotterdam.nl; Schiestraat 18; ☺noon-midnight or later; Ⓜ Rotterdam Centraal)

Bokaal

BAR

31 ⬜ MAP P38, D2

In a *bokaal* (trophy) location at the heart of the enclave around pedestrian Nieuwemarkt and Pannekoekstraat, Bokaal has an indoor bar and a huge all-day sun terrace that heaves with people on summer nights. Beer (craft

Drinking Terraces

In summer, the bars, micro-breweries and *bruin cafés* (traditional Dutch pubs) come into their own, luring locals to their outdoor terraces for a drink or two during sunny afternoons and into sultry evenings. Popular terraces in Centrum include those at Aloha, Biergarten (p49), Bokaal (p49) and De Witte Aap.

and Trappist) is its speciality, with nine on tap, and more than 80 in bottles. There's a food menu, but many take advantage of on-site food trucks. (☎010-720 08 98; www.bokaalrotterdam.nl; Nieuwemarkt 11; ☺11am-1am Sun-Thu, to 2am Fri & Sat; ⊠Meent)

Aloha
BAR

32 🚇 MAP P38, F3

Sustainable, innovative and funky as anything, this bar-cafe in the former Tropicana baths has a large terrace boasting views across the Nieuwe Maas river. Operated by Blue City collective, a group of environmental entrepreneurs, it's a fabulous spot for summer lunches (sandwiches €6 to €9, snacks €5 to €13) or a drink accompanied by the house speciality, mushroom *bitterballen* (deep-fried croquette balls). (☎010-210 81 70; www.alohabar.nl; Maasboulevard 100; ☺noon-11pm Sun-Thu, noon-1am Fri & Sat; Ⓜ Oostplein)

Stirr
COCKTAIL BAR

33 🚇 MAP P38, B4

One of the city's best cocktail bars, Stirr offers an exhilarating package of crazy decor, funky beats and the undivided attention of the bar's legendary whiskered bartenders who will fire a few questions at you and shake up a concoction that you're certain to love. It's on an upper floor; keep your eyes peeled for the door. (www.thestirr.nl; Eendrachtsweg 29b; ☺7pm-1am Sun, Mon, Wed & Thu, 8pm-2am Fri & Sat; Ⓜ Eendrachtsplein, ⊠Museumpark)

De Witte Aap
BROWN CAFE

34 🚇 MAP P38, B4

Anchoring this artist-filled 'hood, the fabulous 'White Monkey' is always crowded with locals. The front opens right up and a huge awning keeps inclement weather at bay. (www.dewitteaap.nl; Witte de Withstraat 78; ☺3pm-4am Sun-Thu, noon-5am Fri & Sat; 🛜; Ⓜ Eendrachtsplein, ⊠Museumpark)

Café LaBru
BAR

35 🚇 MAP P38, B4

Hard-to-find whisky, gin, rum, tequila and craft beers are on the menu at this laid-back drinking den, where live jazz is performed on Wednesday from 9.30pm. Check the Facebook feed for details. (☎010-737 12 05; www.facebook.com/CafeLaBru/; Hartmansstraat 18a; ☺3pm-1am Mon-Thu, 3pm-2am Fri, 2pm-2am Sat, 2pm-1am Sun; Ⓜ Beurs, ⊠Beurs)

Noah

COCKTAIL BAR

36 🚇 MAP P38, E3

There's not a grass skirt in sight, but Europe's oldest skyscraper, the Witte Huis, now has a distinctly Hawaiian flavour thanks to the excellent selection of Tiki cocktails at Noah. Expect funk, soul and R&B DJs (Friday and Saturday only) as well as fiery mai tais. (📞010-213 17 56; www.noahrotterdam.nl; Wijnhaven 3; ⏰4pm-1am Mon-Wed, to 2am Thu, to 4am Fri & Sat; Ⓜ Blaak, 🚊 Blaak)

Toffler

CLUB

37 🚇 MAP P38, B1

Situated in an old pedestrian tunnel that burrows underneath the Weena road, Toffler is a long, narrow club that specialises in the dark arts of techno. (www.toffler.nl;

Weena Zuid 33; ⏰11pm-6am Fri & Sat; Ⓜ Stadhuis, 🚊 Weena, Stadhuis)

Entertainment

Annabel

LIVE MUSIC

38 ⭐ MAP P38, B1

Hosting bands from all genres, Annabel is a choice midsized live-music venue that also hosts regular dance nights. Acts range from hip-hop to pop to electronica. (📞06 2828 9491, WhatsApp only; www.annabel.nu; Schiestraat 20; ⏰8pm-1am Thu, to 2am Fri & Sat; Ⓜ Stadhuis, 🚊 Weena, Pompenburg)

Worm

LIVE MUSIC

39 ⭐ MAP P38, B4

Music here has a try-anything, do-anything vibe. Media mash-

De Witte Aap

ups, queer nights, film screenings, performance art and experimental music are some of the more mundane events. It's part of the Kunstblock (p16) artistic hub. (📞010-476 78 32; www.worm.org; Boomgaardsstraat 71; 🕐3pm-1am Mon-Thu, 2pm-2am Fri & Sat, 2pm-1am Sun, hrs can vary; Ⓜ Beurs, 🚊 Museumpark)

De Doelen
CLASSICAL MUSIC

40 ⭐ MAP P38, A2

Home venue of the renowned Rotterdam Philharmonic Orchestra, this sumptuous 1950s concert hall seating 2200 is also renowned for its jazz and world-music concerts. (📞010-217 17 17; www.dedoelen.nl; Schouwburgplein 50; 🕐ticket office 2-6pm Mon-Fri; Ⓜ Rotterdam Centraal, 🚊 Kruisplein)

Shopping

Groos
FASHION & ACCESSORIES

41 🔒 MAP P38, E1

Its name is revived local slang for 'pride', and this concept store in the Het Industriegebouw creative industries building is clearly proud of the products it stocks, which are conceived, designed and produced in Rotterdam. These include fashion, jewellery, homewares, artworks, books, stationery, music and edibles. (📞010-413 33 44; http://groos. nl; Achterklooster 13; 🕐10am-6pm Tue-Sat, noon-5pm Sun; 🚊 Kipstraat)

De Groene Passage
MARKET

42 🔒 MAP P38, D1

An emporium of eco-conscious and sustainable products, this in-

De Doelen

Summertime Outdoor Cinema

Europe's largest outdoor cinema, **Pleinbioscoop Rotterdam** (http://pleinbioscooprotterdam.nl/; Museumpark; ☉Aug; Ⓜ️Eendrachtsplein, 🚊Museumpark, Vasteland) sets up in Museumpark for most of August. In the evenings, locals of every age pack picnics, rent folding chairs and settle down under the stars to enjoy sessions of arthouse and indie films, Hollywood blockbusters and cinema classics.

door market hosts small business-es selling food, soaps, clothing, homewares, furniture and textiles. If you want to join a tai chi, yoga or Pilates class, or perhaps consult a naturopath, this is the place to come. On Saturdays, organic food stalls sometimes set up on the street outside. (http://degroenepassage.nl/; Mariniersweg 9; ☉8am-8pm Mon-Fri, to 6pm Sat; 🚊Meent)

Rotterdam Tourist Information Gift Shop

GIFTS & SOUVENIRS

43 Ⓐ MAP P38, C3

You can pick up a guide to Rotterdam's architecture or a classy souvenir designed and made in the city (homewares, novelty items, cards, food and more) at the excellent gift shop in the main Tourist Office (p147). (📞010-790 01 85; www.rotterdam.info; Coolsingel 114; ☉9.30am-6pm; Ⓜ️Beurs, 🚊Beurs)

Donner

BOOKS

44 Ⓐ MAP P38, B3

This multifloor place is one of the largest bookshops in the country, with an excellent English-language fiction section and a large selection of travel books. (📞010-413 20 70; www.donner.nl; Coolsingel 119; ☉11am-6pm Mon, 9.30am-6pm Tue-Thu & Sat, 9.30am-9pm Fri, noon-6pm Sun; Ⓜ️Beurs)

Blaak Markt

MARKET

45 Ⓐ MAP P38, D2

This huge street market sprawls across its namesake square east of Markthal. Stalls sell all manner of food, gadgets, clothes, snacks and much more. (☉9am-5pm Tue & Sat; Ⓜ️Blaak, 🚊Blaak)

Explore ◈
Noord

Entering Noord (North), it's immediately apparent that things here don't correspond with the usual norm. Many locals access their 'hood via the Luchtsingel (p59; 'Air Canal'), an elevated pedestrian walkway funded through a crowdsourcing campaign. This links with the Hofbogen (p56), an old elevated railway now housing cafes, boutiques and creative industries. Fortunately, the area retains a multicultural, down-to-earth feel despite these recent incursions.

Visitors will find the neighbourhood easy to explore. Canals and the Hofbogen provide navigational aids, and most points of interest are contained within Schiekade, Bergweg, Zaagmolenstraat and the De Rotte canal. Start by crossing Schiekade via the Luchtsingel and then follow the Hofbogen north before veering northeast. It's a good idea to plan your visit around cafe and restaurant stops, as there are a profusion of these to choose from. You'll find upmarket choices at Station Hofplein (p57), a former train station located next to the Luchtsingel, and affordable neighbourhood eateries (many Italian) elsewhere.

Getting There & Around

Walking Noord is an easy walk from Centraal Station or Centrum

🚋 Lines 8 (direction Kleiweg) or 4 (direction Molenlaan)

Neighbourhood Map on p58

Luchtsingel (p59) IRIS VAN DEN BROEK/SHUTTERSTOCK ©

Walking Tour 🚶

Along the Hofbogen

When stores selling vinyl records and vintage clothes open in a neighbourhood, it's safe to say that the process of gentrification is on the way. And so it is with this neighbourhood northeast of Centraal Station, where new design-driven businesses and hipster cafes seem to open every second day and where the streets reward leisurely exploration.

Walk Facts

Start Luchtsingel, Schiekade access stairs

End Eurotrash United

Length 3.8km; two hours

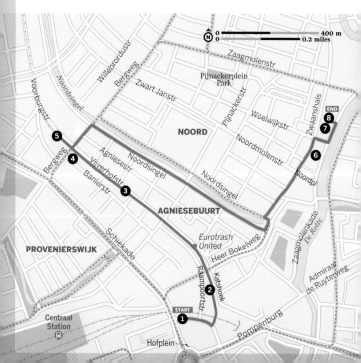

❶ Luchtsingel

This elevated wooden pedestrian bridge (p59) linking Hofplein and Coolsingel with Noord was designed by local studio Zones Urbaines Sensibels (ZUS) and funded by a crowdsourcing campaign.

❷ Station Hofplein

The southern end of the Hofbogen, an arched concrete railway viaduct built in the early 20th-century for the now decommissioned Hofplein line, is known as Station Hofplein. Redeveloped as a retail, dining and entertainment hub, it and the Luchtsingel kick-started Noord's neighbourhood revitalisation.

❸ Man Met Bril

Founder Paul Sharo, the original 'Man with Glasses', has had his vision corrected since setting up this artisan coffee roastery (p62) in 2012, but he has retained the company's spectacles logo alongside its emphasis on supplying direct-trade, freshly roasted beans. The company headquarters here in the Hofbogen serves the 'hood's best coffee.

❹ COPPI

Like their fellow Rotterdammers, residents of the Noord couldn't conceive of life without a bicycle. This hybrid cafe and bike-repair shop (p62) caters to every need of the cycling enthusiast.

❺ Urban Bakery

All that cycling builds healthy appetites, so it's not unusual to see locals parking their bikes and queuing outside this bakery cafe (p61) to get their fix of decadently rich brownies and pretty-as-a-picture cupcakes.

❻ Whiskybase

Many specialist shops have chosen to base their businesses here in Noord. This whisky retailer (p63) is one of them – if you enjoy a dram or two, you'll enjoy browsing its enormous collection.

❼ Lily Scarlet

It's hard to pin down a predominant style when it comes to fashion in Noord, but if there's a overarching theme, it's probably vintage. There are a number of local boutiques catering to lovers of the retro mode but this one (p63) is generally acknowledged as being the best.

❽ Brouwerij Noordt

Every neighbourhood needs at least one local microbrewery. Noord has at least two. Sample one of the 20 brews available on tap at here at Brouwerij Noordt (p62) and then kick on to Eurotrash United (p62) further south if you're in need of an extra libation.

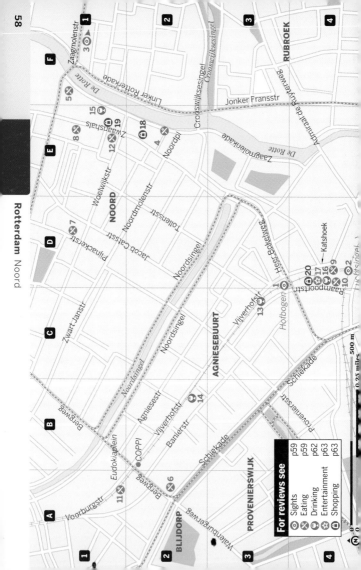

Rotterdam Noord

RUBROEK

Jonker Fransstr

NOORD

Zaagmolenstr

De Rotte

Linker Rotterdamkade

Crooswijksesingel

Crooswijksesingel

Zaagmolenkade

De Rotte

Admiraal de Ruyterweg

Noordpl

Zwaanshals

Woelwijkstr

Noordmolenstr

Tollensstr

Jacob Catsstr

Pijnackerstr

Noordsingel

Noordsingel

Noordsingel

Zwart-Janstr

AGNIESEBUURT

Vijverhofstr

Hofbogen

Heer Bokelweg

Katshoek

Raampoortstr

Schiekade

Schiekade

Voorburgstr

Bergweg

Eudokiaplein

COPPI

Agniesestr

Vijverhofstr

Banierstr

Vijverhofstr

Bergweg

Schiekade

Proveniersstr

PROVENIERSWIJK

BLIJDORP

Walenburgerweg

For reviews see	
⊙ Sights	p59
⊗ Eating	p59
⊗ Drinking	p62
⊗ Entertainment	p63
⊕ Shopping	p63

0.25 miles

500 m

Sights

Hofbogen
AREA

 MAP P58, D3

A cleverly repurposed old railway viaduct, the 1.9km-long Hofbogen houses boutiques, ateliers and other creative spaces that have been built under the viaduct's concrete arches. (www.hofbogen.nl; 🚃 Schiekade, Walenburgerweg)

Luchtsingel
BRIDGE

2 MAP P58, D4

Linking the Schieblock building with the Hofplein and Coolsingel, this yellow, elevated wooden pedestrian bridge was funded by a crowdsourcing campaign. You can buy a plank (with your name on it) that will be part of Luchtsingel. (Air Canal; www.luchtsingel.org; Ⓜ Stadhuis, 🚃 Heer Bokelweg)

Multicultural Hub

Rotterdam is a multicultural city, and nowhere is this more apparent than in Noord. The city's population has been enriched with people from across the globe. The official breakdown is 50% Dutch and 50% from countries including Turkey (8%) and Morocco (7%). Dutch colonies are well represented here too, with 8% of the city's population from Suriname, 4% from the Dutch Caribbean and 2% from Indonesia.

Kralingse Bos & Plas
PARK

3 MAP P58, F1

This bucolic park sits just outside the city centre and offers a delightfully laidback mixture of shaded forest, sparkling waters and manicured grass. It's a peaceful spot where locals come to cycle, sail, row and ride horses. The walk around the lake takes about an hour. Finish off with a cold drink at one of the park's lakeside cafes. (Kralingen Forest and Lake; Kralingse Bos; 🚃 38/Crooswijk)

Eating

Lof der Zoetheid
CAFE €€

4 MAP P58, E2

Its name means 'In Praise of Sweetness', and this stylish cafe certainly serves delicious sweet stuff. Sample the goods in the daily afternoon tea, which includes cake, scones, sandwiches and pies, and tea served from a samovar (Russian tea urn). This is offered from 11.30am to 2pm and 2.30pm to 5pm weekdays and from 11.30am to 2pm and 3pm to 5.30pm weekends. Bookings advised. (📞 010-265 00 70; http://lofderzoetheid.com/; Noordplein 1; afternoon tea €25; ⏱ 10am-5pm Mon & Wed-Fri, to 5.30pm Sat & Sun; 🚃 Zwaanshals)

Bertmans
CAFE €€

5 MAP P58, F1

Asian accents are as pronounced as those from the Mediterranean in the menu at this popular neighbourhood cafe overlooking the serpentine De Rotte canal. The emphasis is on fresh and healthy cafe-style food, accompanied by cold-pressed juices, smoothies, herbal teas or coffee made with locally roasted Giraffe beans. (📞010-844 88 60; https://bertmans. nl; Zaagmolenkade 15; breakfast dishes €7-13, lunch mains €12-16, dinner mains €14-22; 🕐8.45am-10pm Mon-Fri, 9.30am-5.50pm Sat & Sun; 🛜🎇; 🚃Zwaanshals)

Angelo Betti

ITALIAN €

6 🍴 MAP P58, A2

Serving a flavourful array of soft, rich gelato, Angelo Betti has come a long way since its humble beginnings as an ice-cream cart in 1922. Four generations on, it's now a petite family-run restaurant that also sells *delizioso* crispy pizzas. (📞010-465 81 74; www.angelobetti. nl; Schiekade 6b; pizzas €8-16, gelato €5.50-7.50; 🕐4-10pm, closed mid-Jul-mid Aug; 🚃Walenburgerweg)

Tosca

ITALIAN €€

7 🍴 MAP P58, D1

This old-fashioned place has everything you want from a neighbourhood bistro: friendly staff, well-priced food and lovely surrounds including a grapevine-covered terrace overlooking the Brancoplein park. The menu offers Italian classics organised into the traditional *antipasti, primi* (one pasta and one risotto), *secondi* (mainly meat) and *dolci* (all the favourites). (📞010-237 25 89; http:// restauranttosca.nl/; Pijnackerstraat 1;

Lof der Zoetheid (p59)

mains €17-19; ⏱5.30-10pm Wed-Sun;
🍷; 🚇Zwaanshals)

Zino's Urban Bistro   ITALIAN €€

 MAP P58, E1

This neighbourhood eatery is particularly favoured by vegetarians, vegans and gluten-free diners, as there are always suitable choices on the small but tempting menu of modern Italian dishes. The owners also operate the wine shop opposite, and it's possible to buy your own bottle there and enjoy it with your meal. (☎010-466 03 03; www.inourbanbistro.nl; Zwaanshals 265; mains €18-21; ⏱5.30-10pm Wed-Sat; 🍷; 🚇Zwaanshals)

FG   GASTRONOMY €€€

 MAP P58, D4

He's cooked with luminaries including Heston Blumenthal and is certainly Rotterdam's best-known chef, but we're not convinced that François Geurds' menus are impressive enough to justify their hefty prices. However, Michelin disagrees with us (the restaurant has two stars) and so do many of the gastronomes who make their way here. Vegetarian menus can be enjoyed on request. (☎010-425 05 20; www.fgrestaurant.nl; Katshoek 37b, Station Hofplein; 3-course lunch menu Tue-Sat with/without wine pairings €75/45, 5-/6-/7-/8-/9-course menu €125/145/165/185/205; ⏱noon-2pm & 6-9pm Tue-Thu, noon-2pm & 6.30-9.30pm Fri & Sat, closed early-mid-Jan; 🅼Stadhuis, 🚇Heer Bokelweg)

Vroesen Paviljoen

Nestled between the trees of bustling Vroesenpark, north-west of Centraal Station, this wood-framed, glass-fronted **pavilion** (☎010-700 80 30; www.vroesenpaviljoen.nl; Vroesenlaan 60; sandwiches €6-9, mains €14-18; ⏱11am-6pm Mon & Tue, 11am-9pm Wed-Fri, 10am-9pm Sat, 10am-6pm Sun; 🍷🚼; 🅼Blijdorp, 🚇Blijdorp) has a menu offering everything from sandwiches to *stamppot* (potato and vegetable hotpot). It also hosts live music, and yoga and tai chi sessions.

De Jong   EUROPEAN €€€

10 MAP P58, D4

Adventurous chef Jim de Jong wows diners with surprise four-course menus (meat/fish or vegetarian; no à la carte) made from seasonal produce including herbs and flowers from the restaurant's garden. Sadly, the pricey and unimpressive wine pairings let the side down. (☎010-465 79 55; www.restaurantdejong.nl; Raampoortstraat 38; 4-/5-/6-course menus €47/55/62; ⏱6-11pm Wed-Sun; 🍷; 🅼Stadhuis, 🚇Heer Bokelweg)

Urban Bakery   CAFE €

11 MAP P58, A1

If you like brownies, fudge and cupcakes – and who doesn't? – this cafe is for you. Its bakery supplies many of Rotterdam's cafes with

Crazy about Cycling

Rotterdammers love both coffee and cycling, and **COPPI** (Map p58, B2; ☏010-737 17 89; www.coppikoffie.nl; Bergweg 316; ⏰cafe 8.30am-5.30pm Tue-Sun, bike workshop 10am-6pm Tue-Fri & 10am-3pm Sat; 🛜; 🚊Walenburgerweg, Eudokiaplein) caters to both passions. As well as repairing bikes and running a cafe (breakfast dishes €3 to €7, lunch dishes €6 to €9), it holds a cycling tour on the first Sunday of the month (10am, all welcome, helmets compulsory) and hosts special nights when the major cycling tours (Tour, Giro etc) are shown on the big TV screen.

sweet treats. (☏010-751 13 80; www.urbanbakery.nl; Voorburgstraat 217-219; cupcakes €2-2.50; ⏰8.30am-5pm Tue-Sat, 10am-5pm Sun; 🚊Eudokiaplein)

Koen   ICE CREAM €

12 🍴 MAP P58, E1

Koen's head ice cream maker was trained in Italy and it shows: this is excellent artisanal gelato, made with fresh seasonal produce. (☏010-226 59 81; http://ijssalonkoen.nl/; Zwaanshals 317; per scoop €1.30; ⏰noon-10pm Mar-Oct; 🚊Zwaanshals)

Drinking

Eurotrash United   BREWERY

13 🍺 MAP P58, C3

This excellent brewery is the brainchild of Arno Coenen and Iris Roskam, the artists responsible for the enormous mural in Markthal (p40). Fictional characters Kaiser Kuttlipp and Snorella adorn the labels of the brewery's delicious beers, which can be consumed in surroundings that show the artists' unique view on the world.

It attracts students and arty types (☏010-313 49 70; www.eurotrash-united.nl; Vijverhofstraat 10; ⏰3pm-1am; 🚊Heer Bokelweg)

Man Met Bril   COFFEE

14 ☕ MAP P58, B2

Rotterdam's first artisan coffee roastery (there are now 12), Man Met Bril sources direct-trade, 90% organic beans from across the globe and then roasts them in this hip space under a railway viaduct. The on-site cafe offers expertly prepared brews, cakes and sandwiches. Arrive before 10am to take advantage of the generous and dirt-cheap breakfast deal (€6.66). (www.manmetbrilkoffie.nl; Vijverhofstraat 70; ⏰8am-5pm Mon-Fri, 9pm-6pm Sat & Sun; 🛜; 🚊Schiekade Walenburgerweg)

Brouwerij Noordt   BREWERY

15 🍺 MAP P58, E1

Situated in an old fire station (enter through the laneway off Zaagmolenkade), this brewery with its enormous onsite brewing tanks erves 20 tipples on tap. There's in-oor and outdoor seating; payment y card only. (☏010-223 05 66; www. rouwerijnoordt.nl; Zaagmolenkade 46; ⏱taproom 3-7pm Wed-Fri, 2-6pm Sat-un; ☒Zwaanshals)

okaal
CAFE

6 ⓘ MAP P58, D4

ocal Rotterdam products (bread, heese, beer...) are at the heart of okaal but its speciality is brewing otterdam-roasted espresso and lter blends from Giraffe Coffee oasters. The viaduct space is tted out in warm timbers and here are tables on the pavement ut front. (☏010-466 66 65; www. acebook.com/LokaalEspresso/; Raam-oortstraat 34b; ⏱9am-6pm Mon-Fri, ⏱0am-5pm Sat, 11am-5pm Sun; 🛜; ⓂStadhuis, ☒Heer Bokelweg)

Entertainment

ird Jazz Club
LIVE MUSIC

⁊ ✪ MAP P58, D4

lamed after American jazz saxo-honist Charlie 'Bird' Parker, the ity's temple to jazz also stages oul, hip-hop, funk and electronica. io online to see who's playing nd to prepurchase tickets. Its xcellent restaurant serves wood-red pizzas and small plates; the itchen closes at 9.30pm. The lub hosts after-parties during he North Sea Jazz Festival (p21). ttp://bird-rotterdam.nl; Raam-oortstraat 24-28, Station Hofplein; ⏱5.30pm-1am Tue-Thu, to 4am Fri & at; ⓂStadhuis, ☒Heer Bokelweg)

Shopping

Whiskybase
FOOD & DRINKS

18 ⓘ MAP P58, E2

Enjoy a whisky or two? If the answer is yes, this shop with its massive collection of bottles is the place for you. Its Whiskybase Gathering in October attracts up to 2000 whisky drinkers from around the world; check the web-site for details. (☏010-753 17 43; https://whiskybase.com/; Zwaanshals 530; ⏱10.30am-6pm Tue-Fri, to 5pm Sat; ☒Zwaanshals)

Lily Scarlet
VINTAGE

19 ⓘ MAP P58, E1

If you are keen to dress à la mode when in Rotterdam, this vintage shop is a good place to source the appropriate pieces. (☏06 4346 9690; www.lilyscarlet.com; Zwaans-hals 374; ⏱10am-5.30pm Wed-Sat; ☒Zwaanshals)

Clone
MUSIC

20 ⓘ MAP P58, D4

One of the most recent arrivals at Station Hofplein is this relocated Dutch experimental/underground electronic-dance-music record label and vinyl shop. It stocks hard-to-find merchandise (especially T-shirts) too. (☏010-436 95 06; https://clone.nl; Raampoortstraat 12; ⏱10am-6pm Mon-Thu & Sat, 10am-9pm Fri, noon-5pm Sun; ⓂStadhuis, ☒Heer Bokelweg)

Explore ⊕

West

Don't be put off by the fact that this neighbourhood lacks major tourist sights – it compensates with one of the city's few Golden Age enclaves (Delfshaven, p70), a major cafe strip (Nieuwe Binnenweg) and the beautifully landscaped surrounds of Het Park (p74). At the end of the day, local bruin cafés (traditional Dutch pubs) are perfect spots to wind down.

Nieuwe Binnenweg is known for its excellent cafes, so kick off your day's exploration with a coffee here before heading to Coolhaven to visit the Museum Rotterdam '40-'45 NU (p68). Continue east to Het Park, where you can zoom to the top of the Euromast (p75), wander through the park and enjoy lunch on one of the deck chairs at Parqiet (p77). Afterwards, explore the historic enclave of Delftshaven, sample the house brews at Stadsbrouwerij De Pelgrim (p79), enjoy dinner nearby and then consider kicking on to the oh-so-fashionable Suicide Club (p79) to drink and dance the night away.

Getting There & Around

🚇 Lines A and B (direction Schiedam Centrum) and C (direction De Akkers).

🚋 Lines 4 (direction Marconiplein) and 8 (direction Spangen).

⛴ Watertaxi docks at Euromast or Sint-Jobshaven/Mullerpier.

Neighbourhood Map on p72

Delfshaven (p70) PORTUMEN/SHUTTERSTOCK ©

Top Sights 📷
Van Nelle Fabriek

One of only 10 World Heritage–listed sights in the Netherlands, this former coffee, tea and tobacco factory is a gleaming triumph of modernist architecture. Built between 1925 and 1931 on the banks of a canal in Rotterdam's inner northwest, it is widely acknowledged to be one of the global icons of 20th-century industrial architecture. The factory operated until the 1990s and now houses creative industries.

◎ MAP P72, A1

Van Nelle Factory

www.vannellefabriek.com

Van Nelleweg 1

🚆 38 & B9 from Centraal Station

The Architectural Vision

Conceived as an 'ideal factory' where interior working spaces evolved according to need and where daylight was used to provide healthy and enjoyable working conditions, the factory became a symbol of interwar modernity as soon as it opened. Architects Johannes Brinkman and Leendert van der Vlugt, Rotterdam-based exponents of the *Nieuwe Bouwen* (Dutch functionalist) movement, designed a streamlined concrete structure sheathed in a massive curtain wall of glass and steel. Its three main sections — one for tobacco, another for coffee and a third for tea — are linked with service areas containing washrooms, stairs and lifts. All three are connected by distinctive elevated bridges.

Notable Features

Within the factory complex, there is an office building whose sinuous form mirrors the curve of the entrance driveway, a circular tea room on top of the tobacco section, separate male and female staircases (to prevent staff fraternisation) and an on-site electricity plant.

Nearby

The orange-and-blue low bunker to the east of the factory is the De Schie Penitentiary, designed by CJM Weeber and constructed between 1985 and 1989. Its startlingly vivid colour scheme is in stark contrast to its dark function.

★ **Top Tips**

o Though closed to the public during the week, the factory sometimes offers guided tours on weekends (adult/child under 13 €8.50/5); check the website for details. Urban Guides (p19) also runs one-hour guided tours (per person €15) most Saturdays and Sundays (book ahead).

o After visiting the factory, you may be inspired to visit Huis Sonneveld (p34), also designed by Brinkman and Van der Vlugt.

✕ **Take a Break**

Walk south alongside the Delftshaveneschie canal to reach historic Delftshaven, where you can enjoy a beer at Stadsbrouwerij De Pelgrim (p79) or De Oude Sluis (p79).

Top Sights 📷
Museum Rotterdam '40-'45 NU

Sheltered under a bridge on Coolhaven, this small but excellent museum documents life in Rotterdam during WWII and offers an eight-minute immersive multimedia experience outlining the terror and destruction caused by the bombing of Rotterdam on 14 May 1940, when 54 German aircraft dropped 1300 bombs on the city over a 13-minute period.

◎ **MAP P72, E5**

www.40-45nu.nl

Coolhaven 375

adult/child 4-17
€7.50/2.50

🕑10am-5pm Sat, 11am-5pm Sun

Ⓜ Coolhaven

The Exhibition

Artefact-driven displays in huge glass cases focus on all aspects of the wartime experience, with tales of optimism and bravery interspersing many sad stories. The displays are well labelled in English and topics addressed include the German bombardment, the great fire that followed, the Germans' unconscionable treatment of Rotterdam's Jewish community (and the heroic efforts by some non-Jewish locals to shelter Jewish neighbours), local resistance to the German occupation and the liberation of the city by Canadian troops on 8 May 1945.

Lesser-Known Stories

The 1940 blitz wasn't the only bombing that Rotterdammers were to be subjected to during WWII. Displays tell of how Allied air forces carried out a number of raids during the time that the Germans were in control of the city (1940–45), including bombing strategic installations in and around the port. On 31 March 1943, one of these raids went horribly wrong, when the US Army Air Forces mistakenly bombed a residential area, killing hundreds of men, women and children. This is sometimes referred to as the 'Forgotten Bombardment'.

Foyer Display

A thought-provoking and depressing display in the foyer reminds visitors that many other cities have undergone experiences such as Rotterdam's in recent times.

★ Top Tips

o To garner an understanding of what the city looked like before being devastated in WWII, visit Museum Rotterdam (p40) in Centrum before coming here.

o During Dutch school holidays, the museum is open 10am to 5pm Tuesday to Friday as well as weekends; check the website for holiday dates.

✕ Take a Break

The Nieuwe Binnenweg cafe strip is close by – enjoy a coffee, brunch or lunch at Urban Espresso Bar (p75), Lilith (p79) or La Zia Maria (p78).

Het Park, east of the museum, is home to popular Parqiet (p77) and De Ballentent (p79); both have indoor and outdoor seating and are great spots for lunch or a drink.

Walking Tour 🥾

Delfshaven

One of the few neighbourhoods in Rotterdam to escape bombardment during WWII, this historic port area retains many traditional features, including a reconstructed windmill, churches and bruin cafés (traditional Dutch pubs). The pace of city life is slower here than in many other neighbourhoods, particularly on weekdays. On weekends, visitors from around the city descend.

Walk Facts

Start Pool Café
End De Oude Sluis
Length 900m; one hour

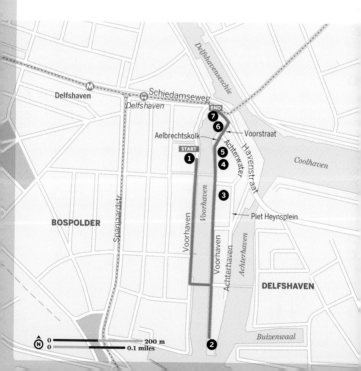

❶ Pool Café

Fancy a game of pool or darts? You can do that *and* enjoy a beer and burger at this **pool hall** (☎010-425 77 16; www.poolcafedelfshaven.nl; Aelbrechtskolk 45b; ⊗noon-midnight Mon-Thu, to 1am Fri & Sat, to 9pm Sun; ☐Delftshaven). There are plenty of tables, and regular tournaments too. You're bound to find someone to enjoy a game with.

❷ Windmill

This reconstructed 18th-century **windmill** (Voorhaven 210; admission free) overlooks the water at Delfshaven. It still mills grain; unfortunately the interior is closed to the public.

❸ Restaurant Frits

Follow Voorhaven south before crossing the canal and heading north again, to Restaurant Frits (p77). The canal-house setting of this restaurant is lovely, but that's not the main reason why locals flock here. The real attraction is the amazing-value eight-course surprise menu with ingredients from the restaurant's kitchen garden. You'll need to book in advance to score a table.

❹ Oude of Pelgrimvaderskerk

The Pilgrims prayed at this 15th-century church (p74) before leaving the Netherlands for America aboard the *Speedwell* on 1 August 1620. Locals worship here on Sundays, and also attend the regular cultural events – often musical evenings – that are hosted at other times.

❺ Stadsbrouwerij De Pelgrim

This brewery (p79) produces a wide variety of seasonal beers, but locals know that they can rely on its best-known tipple, the Mayflower Tripel, to be available year-round. In winter, the historic taproom is a cosy spot; in summer, the sunny canalside terrace beckons.

❻ Petra Jongmans

There's an artisanal flavour to Delfshaven, and ateliers in the neighbourhood include this canalside working and retail space where jeweller Petra Jongmans (p81) creates stylish silver jewellery.

❼ De Oude Sluis

Keeping the tradition of the *bruin café* alive and well in Delfshaven, this pub (p79) has a terrace with postcard-perfect views down the canal to the windmill. The many regulars enjoy drinking beer, chatting with their neighbours and listening to occasional live music.

A De Schie Penitentiary

1 Van Nelle Fabriek

Schuttevaerweg

Roel Langer Park

2 SPANGEN

Delfshavensche

Beukelsdijk

V Citerssstr

3 Mathenesserdijk

Vierambachtsstr

Mathenesserweg

Mathenesserlaan

NIEUWE WESTEN

Spangesekade

Albrechtskade

Delfshavensche

4 Marconiplein

TUSSENDIJKEN

Schiedam (2.5km)

Schiedamseweg

Delfshaven

Havenstraat

Rochusser

5 Vierhavenstr

Hudsonstr

14

Aelbrechtskolk

Stadsbrouwerij De Pelgrim

Oude of Pelgrimvaderskerk

20

2

Achterwat

8

9

Piet Heynsple

BOSPOLDER

Spanjaardstr

Voorhaven

Voorhaven Achterhaven

DELFSHAV

For reviews see

◉ Top Sights	p66
◎ Sights	p74
⊗ Eating	p75
🍷 Drinking	p79
✪ Entertainment	p80
🛍 Shopping	p81

6 Middenkous

◎N 0 ————— 500 m
    0 ————— 0.25 miles

SCHIEMOND

A   **B**   **C**   **D**

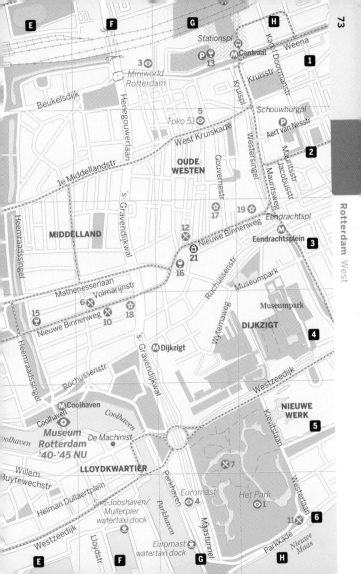

E
F
G
H

1

Stationspl

P

13

M Centraal

Karel Doormanstr

Weena

Kruispl

Kruisstr

Schouwburgpl

3

Miniworld
Rotterdam

Beukelsdijk

Henegouwerlaan

5

Toko 51

West Kruiskade

Aert van Nesstr

P

Mauritsstr
Jacobusstr

Mauritsweg

2

1e Middellandstr

**OUDE
WESTEN**

Gouvernestr

Westersingel

s'- Gravendijkwal

17

19

Eendrachtspl

Heemraadssingel

MIDDELLAND

12

Nieuwe Binnenweg

21

16

M Eendrachtsplein

3

Rochussenstr

Museumpark

Mathenesserlaan

Volmarijnstr

Museumpark

DIJKZIGT

4

15

6

Nieuwe Binnenweg

10

18

Wytemaweg

Rochussenstr

s'- Gravendijkwal

M Dijkzigt

Heemraadssingel

Westzeedijk

M Coolhaven

Coolhaven

**NIEUWE
WERK**

5

Coolhaven

Kievitslaan

Coolhaven

**Museum
Rotterdam
'40-'45 NU**

De Machinist

Willem

LLOYDKWARTIER

Parkhaven

7

Buytewechstr

Helman Dullaertplein

Sint-Jobshaven/
Mullerpier
watertaxi dock

Parkhaven

Parklaan

Euromast

4

Het Park

1

11

6

Westzeedijk

Lloydstr

Euromast
watertaxi dock

Maastunnel

Parkkade

Nieuwe
Maas

Westerlaan

E
F
G
H

Sights

Het Park   PARK

1 ◉ MAP P72, H6

Landscaped in English-garden style, this park was established in 1852 and is much loved by locals, who come here to jog, picnic, barbecue, cycle, kick around footballs and enjoy a coffee, drink or meal at charming Parqiet (p77), a cafe with deck-chair seating on the lawn. (👪; 🚋Euromast/Erasmus MC)

Oude of Pelgrimvaderskerk   CHURCH

2 ◉ MAP P72, D5

The Pilgrims prayed at this church one last time before leaving the Netherlands for America aboard the *Speedwell* on 1 August 1620. They could barely keep the leaky boat afloat and, in England, eventually transferred to the *Mayflower* – the rest is history. The building dates from 1417, but was extensively rebuilt in the late 16th century. Inside is an 1890 outbuilding housing a memorial to the Pilgrims. (Pilgrim Fathers Church 📞010-477 41 56; www.oudeofpelgrim vaderskerk.nl; Aelbrechtskolk 22; ⏰noon-6pm Sat & every 2nd Fri; 🚋Delfshaven)

Miniworld Rotterdam   MUSEUM

3 ◉ MAP P72, F1

The Dutch love of the world in miniature is celebrated at the vast Miniworld, a ginormous, 535 sq metre, 1:87 scale model railroad re-creating contemporary Rotterdam, with day and night simulation. (📞010-240 05 01; www. miniworldrotterdam.com; Weena 745; adult/child 3-11 €11.50/7.50; ⏰weekday hrs vary, 10am-5pm Sat & Sun; 👪; Ⓜ Rotterdam Centraal, 🚋Centraal)

The Pilgrims

In 1620, a group of English Calvinists who had split from the Anglican Church and migrated to Leiden to flee religious persecution determined to continue their journey and establish new lives in America. Travelling from Leiden to the port at Delfshaven, they purchased a sailing ship called the *Speedwell*, prayed for a safe journey at the Oude of Pelgrimvaderskerk and set off to rendezvous at Southhampton with another ship heading to America, the *Mayflower*. Unfortunately, the leaky *Speedwell* didn't live up to its name; after two unsuccessful attempts to get underway, both ships sailed back to Southampton, where some of the *Speedwell* passengers boarded the much more seaworthy *Mayflower* and sailed, as it were, into history as the Pilgrims.

Euromast
VIEWPOINT

4 ◎ MAP P72, G6

Designed by HA Maaskant as a landmark and built between 1958 and 1960, the 185m-high Euromast offers unparalleled 360-degree views of Rotterdam from its 100m-high observation deck, or from its rotating glass Euroscoop elevator, which goes right to the top of the mast. (www.euromast.nl; Parkhaven 20; adult/child €9.75/6.25; ⏰9.30am-11pm Apr-Sep, 10am-11pm Oct-Mar; 🚇Euromast/Erasmus MC)

Toko 51
CULTURAL CENTRE

5 ◎ MAP P72, G2

A melting pot for local creatives, this space hosts pop-up exhibitions, stores, gigs and get-togethers. (📞06 8359 6809; www.

facebook.com/cretopiarotterdam/; West Kruiskade 51; ⏰Fri & Sat, hrs vary; 🚇Kruisplein)

Eating

Urban Espresso Bar
CAFE €

6 ✖ MAP P72, F4

Could this be Rotterdam's best cafe? The coffee here is definitely a cut above most of its competitors (Giraffe beans, expert baristas), as is the food (artisan breads and pastries, house-baked cakes, global flavours, organic ingredients). We can highly recommend the *tosties* (toasted sandwiches), soups and burgers, and we always enjoy chatting with fellow customers at the communal table. Cash only. (UEB West; 📞010-477 01 88; www.urbanespressobar.nl; Nieuwe

Oude of Pergrimvaderskerk

The Rotterdam Blitz

It's true to say that a single event has largely shaped modern Rotterdam. On 14 May 1940, near the beginning of WWII a squadron of 90 Luftwaffe (German air force) planes dropped over 1000 bombs on the city, destroying buildings and setting off a firestorm that levelled the medieval city centre and many other neighbourhoods. When the fires eventually died down, Rotterdammers were faced with an immense task: surviving the war and rebuilding both their city and their lives.

Devastation

Combined, the bombings and fires killed more than 900 people. At least 24,000 homes were destroyed, as were 24 churches, over 2000 shops, 775 warehouses and 62 schools. Around 80,000 Rotterdammers were made homeless. Photographs taken at the time show the badly damaged Laurenskerk (the city's main church; Map p38, D2) and the Stadhuis (City Hall; Map p38, C2) as two of only a few major buildings left standing.

The Impact

Rotterdam was the country's industrial engine room and major port. With most of the city destroyed and the Germans threatening to subject Utrecht to the same treatment, the Dutch Government felt that it had no choice but to surrender. It did so on 15 May, one day after the blitz.

Rebuilding the City

Within four days of the bombings, the city architect, WG Witteveen, was asked to draw up plans to rebuild the city. His scheme, which proposed reconstructing the historical urban structure of the city, received a cool reception when he presented it to the authorities. His assistant Cornelis van Traa soon assumed direction of the reconstruction process.

The new city that Van Traa envisaged had a completely new spacial layout and an efficient traffic plan. Houses were built on the outskirts of the city in new residential areas that featured high-rise housing, parks and roads. The city centre gained high-rise commercial and office buildings, as well as innovations such as Lijnbaan, the global prototype for the modern pedestrianised strip-mall. The era of innovation and experimentation in urban design and architecture had arrived, and continues in Rotterdam today.

Binnenwag 263; sandwiches €5-6, mains €7-9; ☺9am-6pm Mon-Sat, 10am-6pm Sun; 🛜📶; 🚃Claes de Vrieselaan)

Parqiet

CAFE €

🍴 MAP P72, G5

The wild flowers in Kilner jars, terrace seating and striped deckchairs on the front lawn all contribute to the charm of this cafe in a former coach house in Het Park (p74). Dishes are light and fresh, with plenty of vegetarian options, and baristas get the best out of the Marzocco espresso machine using freshly roasted Man Met Bril beans. (📞06 5100 1606; www.parqiet.nl; Baden Powelllaan 20; breakfast dishes €5-9, sandwiches €6-9; ☺9am-6pm; 🛜📶; 🚃Euromast/Erasmus MC)

Restaurant Frits

MODERN EUROPEAN €€

8 🍴 MAP P72, D5

Inside a pretty Delfshaven canal house, with an intimate split-level, dark-timber interior, Frits serves an astounding-value eight-course surprise menu using ingredients from its own kitchen garden. Although there's no choice on the night (and no à la carte), chef Robbert van Gammeren skilfully adapts to dietary requirements (gluten-free, vegetarian, allergies) with advance notice. Reservations are essential. (📞010-477 30 25; www.facebook.com/restaurant frits/; Piet Heynsplein 25; 8-course menu €40; ☺6-10pm Thu-Sun; 🚃Delfshaven)

Parqiet

't Ouwe Bruggetje
MODERN EUROPEAN €€€

9 🍴 MAP P72, D5

This long-operating restaurant has an atmospheric timber-panelled interior, as well as seating by the iron-framed drawbridge out front and on a floating terrace on the canal. Dining is by set 'surprise' menu only – these range from two to five courses. Dessert (€8.50) or cheese (€10) aren't included. A seven-course surprise menu with aperitif, wine and coffee costs €85. (📞010-477 34 99; www.historisch-delfshaven.nl; Voorhaven 6; set menus €30-48; ⏰6-10pm Wed-Sat, 5-10pm Sun; 🚇Delfshaven)

La Zia Maria
ITALIAN €

10 🍴 MAP P72, F4

There is limited table seating at this old-fashioned and aromatic deli, but if you don't manage to snag a sit-down spot, it's still a fabulous place to pick up Italian specialities such as *formaggi* (cheese), *salumi* (cold cuts) and antipasti for a canal-side picnic. The chef uses Rustichella d'Abruzzo artisan pasta to make his traditional dishes, which are satisfyingly filling. (📞010-270 92 95; www.facebook.com/LaZiaMaria Rotterdam/; Nieuwe Binnenweg 222a; panini €7-8, pastas €9-11; ⏰noon-7pm Mon, 11am-7pm Tue-Fri, 10am-6pm Sat; 🚇's-Gravendijkwal)

KINO (p80)

De Ballentent

PUB FOOD €€

🍴 😊 MAP P72, H6

Rotterdam's best waterfront pub is also a great spot for a meal. Dine on one of two terraces or inside. Mussels, schnitzels and more line the menu but the real speciality here are *ballen,* huge homemade meatloafy meatballs. The plain ones are tremendous, but go for the house style with a piquant sauce of fresh peppers, mushrooms and more. (🖉010-436 04 62; www.deballentent.nl; Parkkade 1; mains €11-17; 🕙9am-11pm Mon-Fri, from 10am Sat & Sun; 🚊Kievitslaan)

Lilith

CAFE €

12 😊 MAP P72, G3

The front terrace at this neighbourhood favourite is inevitably crowded in sunny weather, and queuing for tables is not unknown. Breakfast is the busiest time, when eggs (Benedict, scrambled, Florentine etc) and vegan treats such as mushrooms or avocado on toast reign supreme. (http://lilithcoffee.com/; Nieuwe Binnenweg 125h; breakfast dishes €4-11; 🕙8am-6pm; 🛜🪑; 🚊Bloemkwekersstraat)

Drinking

Suicide Club

COCKTAIL BAR

13 😊 MAP P72, G1

Situated on the top floor of the iconic and monolithic Groothandelsgebouw building, this rooftop bar is where the beau monde comes to mingle. Expect cush-

Stadsbrouwerij De Pelgrim

The sight of bubbling copper vats and the heady scent of hops greets you at this vintage **brewery** (Map p72, D5; 🖉010-477 11 89; www.pelgrimbier.nl; Aelbrechtskolk 12; 🕙noon-midnight Wed-Sat, to 10pm Sun; 🚊Delfshaven) abutting the Oude of Pelgrimvaderskerk. Here you can take a voyage through an array of seasonal and standard beers such as the popular Mayflower Tripel in the bar, canal-side terrace or courtyard. A tasting flight of five beers costs €5.

ioned cabanas, cutting-edge DJs (Friday and Saturday) and can't-stop-talking-about-them views. Try the Bamboo Chute (vodka, gin, lemon, coconut, pandan and cinnamon). (🖉010-846 87 97; www.thesuicideclub.nl; Stationsplein 45, 8th fl; 🕙4pm-2am Sun, Wed & Thu, to 5am Fri & Sat; Ⓜ Rotterdam Centraal, 🚊Centraal)

De Oude Sluis

BROWN CAFE

14 😊 MAP P72, D5

The view up the canal from the terrace stretches to Delfshaven's windmill at this *bruin café*, which has been a popular neighbourhood spot since 1912. There's occasional live music and a good choice of beer on tap and by bottle. (🖉010-477 30 68; www.cafedeoudesluis.nl;

De Machinist

Occupying a handsome brown-brick building where stoking and other ship-related trades were once taught, hybrid restaurant, bar and club **De Machinist** (Map p72, F5; ☑010-477 57 00; www.demachinist.nl; Willem Buytewechstraat 45; ⏲11am-11pm Sun-Thu, to midnight Fri & Sat; ☒Willem Buytewechstraat) hosts regular live comedy performances and quiz nights. In July it stages North Sea Jazz Festival (p21) gigs. The outdoor terrace overlooking Coolhaven is a pleasant spot for a coffee, drink or meal.

Havenstraat 7; ⏲noon-1am Mon-Thu, noon-2am Fri, 2pm-2am Sat, 2pm-1am Sun; ☒Delfshaven)

Café Steijn   PUB

15 ☒ MAP P72, E4

The streetside seating at this popular neighbourhood pub overlooks the Heemraadspark and canal, and is a lovely spot to while away an afternoon. There's pub grub on offer, too. (☑010-845 30 86; https://facebook.com/CafeSteijn/; Nieuwe Binnenweg 345b; ⏲11am-11pm; ☒Heemraadsplein)

Wester Paviljoen   GRAND CAFE

16 ☒ MAP P72, G3

The sunny terrace is the main draw at this old-fashioned grand cafe. (☑010-436 26 45; http://westerpaviljoen.nl/; Mathenesserlaan 157; ⏲8am-1am Mon-Fri, 9am-1am Sat & Sun; ☒Mathenesserlaan)

Entertainment

KINO   CINEMA

17 ☆ MAP P72, G3

Since the ribbon was cut in 1909, this legendary Rotterdam cinema has had bit-part roles as a music venue, a theatre and even as a hospital. Renovated in 2016, when it reopened as KINO, it now houses four cinemas, a bar and a restaurant. The film selection tends to veer towards the daring. (☑010-268 11 60; www.kinorotterdam.nl; Gouvernestraat 129-133; ⏲10am-1am Sun-Thu, to 2am Fri & Sat; ☒Bloemkwekersstraat)

Dizzy   LIVE MUSIC

18 ☆ MAP P72, F4

Live acts perform most nights at this decades-old jazz cafe, and can include anything from cool jazz to blues-tinged sets, funk and Latin. The whisky collection is renowned (☑010-477 30 14; www.dizzy.nl; 's-Gravendijkwal 127; ⏲noon-1am Tue-Thu, to 2am Fri & Sat, to 11pm Sun; ☒'s-Gravendijkwal)

Rotown   LIVE MUSIC

19 ☆ MAP P72, H3

A smooth bar, a dependable live-rock venue, an agreeable restaurant and a popular meeting place. The musical program features new local talent, established international acts and crossover experiments. (☎010-436 26 42; www.rotown.nl; Nieuwe Binnenweg 17-19; ⏰noon-2am Sun-Thu, 11am-3am Fri & Sat; Ⓜ Eendrachtsplein, 🚊Eendrachtsplein)

Shopping

Petra Jongmans   JEWELLERY

20 🅐 MAP P72, D5

Local artisan Petra Jongman creates sleek and extremely attractive silver jewellery at this canal-side atelier and shop in Delfshaven. She also runs occasional jewellery-making workshops. (☎06 41 04 31 46; www.petrajongmans.nl; Voorstraat 7; ⏰11am-4pm Wed & Thu; 🚊Delfshaven)

Schorem   FASHION & ACCESSORIES

21 🅐 MAP P72, G3

Styled on the barbershops of old, Schorem offers traditional gel-thick haircuts like pompadours, flattops and contours. However, it's the atmosphere that makes this place special as no-nonsense Rotterdammers shoot the breeze with a beer whilst waiting to have their ears lowered. The shop also sells vinyl, books and posters as well as hair putty, beard foams and Reuzel aftershave. (☎010-720 08 04; www.schorembarbier.nl; Nieuwe Binnenweg 104; ⏰10am-5pm Mon-Sat; 🚊Bloemkwekersstraat)

Explore ⊕

Zuid

Since city authorities initiated major programs in the 1980s to redevelop the docks at Kop van Zuid (South Bank) and the red-light district on the Katendrecht peninsula, these neighbourhoods south of the Nieuwe Maas have become some of the city's most vibrant. They're also home to many of Rotterdam's most notable contemporary buildings.

Easily accessed by metro, tram or watertaxi, Rotterdam Zuid can also be accessed by foot via two bridges: the Erasmusbrug (aka 'The Swan'; p89) and red Willemsbrug. To spend a rewarding day here, start by walking over the Willemsbrug, crossing Noordereiland and heading southeast through Kop van Zuid to Wilhelminapier, where you can visit the Nederlands Fotomuseum (p88), admire the buildings along Wilhelminakade and pause for a drink on the terrace of historic Hotel New York (p93). Afterwards, continue south to Katendrecht to visit the Fenix Food Factory (p90) and then stay to eat and drink at one of the venues around Deliplein.

Getting There & Around

Ⓜ Lines D (direction De Akkers) and E (direction Slinge); alight at Wilhelminaplein for Kop van Zuid and Feijenoord, and at Rijnhaven for Katendrecht

⚓ Several watertaxi docks on Wilhelminapier and Katendrecht

🚋 Lines 20, 23 and 25 to Wilhelminaplein, Lodewijk Pincoffsweg or Vuurplaat.

Neighbourhood Map on p86

Walking Tour 🚶

The Old Red Light District

Often referred to as de Kaap (the Cape), Katen-drecht was once Rotterdam's red-light district. In recent decades, an extraordinary transformation has occurred here, with old port-related commercial and industrial buildings being demolished and replaced with new, predominantly social, housing. The streets around Deliplein have morphed into a fashionable entertainment hub.

Walk Facts

Start Rijnhaven Bridge
End City Stories Centre
Length 1.1km; one hour

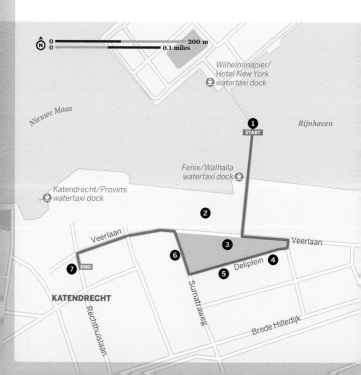

❶ Rijnhaven Bridge

The exciting development of Katendrecht was facilitated by construction of this bridge over Rijnhaven, which provides a pedestrian and cycling link with Wilhelminapier. Made of wood and stainless-steel mesh, it is adorned with padlocks ('lovelocks') affixed by local couples asserting undying love for each other.

❷ Fenix Food Factory

A shopping destination, eating and drinking precinct and exemplary example of entrepreneurial enterprise, this indoor food market (p90) in a shabby warehouse is one of the city's go-to destinations, offering everything from a craft brewery to a bakery and coffee roastery. On summer evenings, young crowds spill out onto the dock overlooking Rijnhaven and the Wilhelminapier highrises.

❸ Deliplein

A triangular-shaped plaza fringed by trees, Deliplein is a popular entertainment precinct lined with cafes, bars, restaurants and boutiques. Most of the eateries here are at the budget end of the price scale (CEO Baas van Het Vlees – p91 – being a notable exception), making it a popular spot with students and bohemian types.

❹ Tattoo Bob

Tattooing in Katendrecht since 1968, this parlour (p95) is where many locals come to get inked and pierced. Known throughout the country, the business has changed a lot since the days when it was geared towards drunken sailors.

❺ Café De Ouwehoer

Cosy and arty in equal measure, this much-loved bar (p92) on Deliplein offers an excellent selection of beer and whisky, and plenty of chances to chat with regulars while you enjoy your drink.

❻ Theater Walhalla

Named after a louche pre-WWII dance hall where sailors made the most of their shore leave, this pocket-sized theatre (p94) now stages cabaret, music and theatre acts.

❼ Verhalenhuis Kaap Belvédère

Dedicated to collecting, studying and exhibiting intangible heritage, the City Stories Centre (p89) hosts changing exhibitions and oral history audiovisuals recounting the personal stories of individuals and communities within the contemporary city, and particularly in Katendrecht. Locals congregate at the cafe on the ground floor.

Rotterdam Zuid

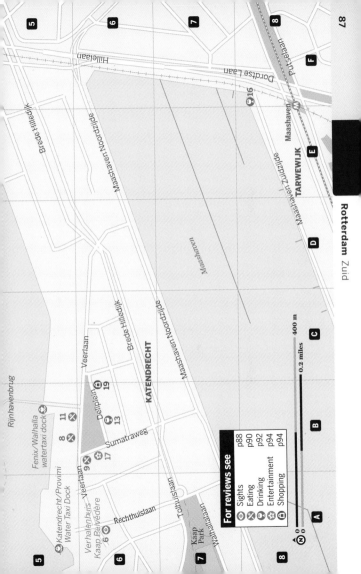

Sights

De Rotterdam ARCHITECTURE

1 MAP P86, C3

Designed by OMA, whose star architect Rem Koolhaas is a Pritzker-winning local hero, this 'vertical city' with its three interconnected towers was completed in 2013 and is the city's most acclaimed contemporary building. It incorporates Rotterdam city council offices, apartments, the nhow hotel (p142) and cocktail bar (p93), and restaurants including HMB (p91). (www.derotterdam.nl; Wilhelminakade 177; **M**Wilhelminaplein)

Nederlands Fotomuseum MUSEUM

2 MAP P86, C3

This national institution has a collection of over five million photographic images, and its upstairs gallery highlights curated selections from this incredible resource. The work of major Dutch photographers such as Ed van der Elsken, Aart Klein and Cas Oorthuys often features. The ground-floor galleries host temporary exhibitions of the work of big-name photographers from the Netherlands and around the world. (☏010-203 04 05; www.nederlandsfotomuseum.nl; Wilhelminakade 332; adult/student 18-25/child under 18 €12/6/free; ◷11am-5pm Tue-Sun; **M**Wilhelminaplein)

Cruise Terminal ARCHITECTURE

3 MAP P86, C3

Much of the Holland-America Line infrastructure in Rotterdam was destroyed during the 1940s bombings, and replaced directly after the war. This terminal building with its six distinctive shell roofs and fully glazed side elevations was one of them. Designed by Brinkman,

Navigating Rotterdam Zuid

Zuid's three main precincts – Kop van Zuid, Feijenoord and Katendrecht – have radically different building stock and atmospheres. Kop van Zuid is a carefully curated modern mashup of office buildings, hotels, housing and cultural institutions; its Wilhelminapier enclave is where you will find a number of the city's most architecturally significant buildings. Feijenoord is home to working docks, parks, housing stock, Feyenoord's football stadium De Kuip (The Tub) and corporate headquarters including the distinctive Unilever Building, which cantilevers out over the Nieuwe Maas and is often referred to as *De Brug* (The Bridge). Katendrecht, linked to Wilhelminapier by the Rijnhaven Bridge, has a vibrant entertainment and shopping precinct around Deliplein but is predominantly residential, with plenty of high-quality public housing.

Erasmusbrug with De Rotterdam and KPN Telecom Headquarters (p90)

Van den Broek & Bakema, it was completed in 1949. (Wilhelminakade 699; M Wilhelminaplein)

Erasmusbrug BRIDGE

4 ⊙ MAP P86, B1

A symbol of the city, this graceful pylon bridge dubbed 'the Swan' was designed by architect Ben van Berkel and completed in 1996. It spans 802m across the Maas river and can be both walked, cycled and driven across. (M Wilheminaplein)

Maastoren ARCHITECTURE

5 ⊙ MAP P86, E1

Commissioned as the Dutch headquarters of Deloitte, 165m Maastoren was designed by Dam & Partners and was the tallest

building in the Netherlands when it was completed in 2009. Its durable heating and cooling system uses water from the Maas river and energy storage in the soil to reduce the building's carbon footprint. (Maas Tower; Wilhelminakade 1; M Wilhelminaplein)

Verhalenhuis Kaap Belvédère CULTURAL CENTRE

6 ⊙ MAP P86, A6

Rotterdam's City Stories Centre is dedicated to collecting, studying and exhibiting the city's intangible heritage. Changing exhibitions and oral history audiovisuals on the second and third floors of an 1894 building in Katendrecht recount the personal stories of individuals and communities within contemporary, multicultural Rotterdam. There's a cafe on the ground floor. (📞010 720 09 97; www.verhalenhuisbelvedere.nl; Rechthuislaan 1; admission free; 🕐11am-6pm Fri-Sun; Ⓜ Rijnhaven)

KPN Telecom Headquarters

ARCHITECTURE

7 ◎ MAP P86, C2

Designed by celebrated architect Renzo Piano and opened in 2000, the bizarre KPN Telecom headquarters building leans at a sharp angle, seemingly resting on a long pole. The six-degree lean is the same as the Leaning Tower of Pisa's – a suitably Italian reference by one of Italy's greatest architects. (Toren op Zuid; Wilhelminakade 123; Ⓜ Wilhelminaplein)

Eating

Fenix Food Factory

MARKET €

8 🍴 MAP P86, B5

Almost everything in this vast former warehouse is made locally and sold by entrepreneurs making their mark on the food scene. They include Booij Kaasmakers (p94) selling cheese, milk, yoghurt, eggs, Cider Cider, Jordy's Bakery (bread and baked goods), Stielman Koffiebranders (coffee roasters), Stroop Rotterdam (*stroopwafels*, or syrup waffles), Kaapse Brouwers (craft brewery), Firma Bijten (meat) and De Westlandse Tuin (fruit and vegies). (www.fenixfoodfactory.nl; Veerlaan 19d; 🕐10am-7pm Tue-Thu, to 8pm Fri, to 6pm Sat,

KPN Telecom Headquarters (right)

Hotel New York

The former headquarters of the Holland-America passenger-ship line now houses **Hotel New York** (Map p86, B4; ☏010-439 05 55; www.hotelnewyork.nl; Koninginnenhoofd 1; Ⓜ Wilhelminaplein). It was designed by J Muller, Droogleever Fortuyn and CB van der Trak, and was built in stages between 1901 and 1919. Decommissioned as an office in the 1970s when the company relocated its business to Seattle in the USA, it was converted into a hotel in the 1990s and included on the national heritage register in 2000. The art nouveau–influenced building with its two whimsical clock towers is now a much-loved city icon. Apart from accommodation, Hotel New York houses several restaurants and bars (p93).

noon-6pm Sun, individual stall hrs vary; ✈ ♨; Ⓜ Rijnhaven)

CEO Baas van Het Vlees
STEAK €€€

 9 🍴 MAP P86, B6

Meat lovers should be sure to book a table at Rotterdam's best steakhouse. Working in their open kitchen, chefs cook spectacular cuts of beef to order. We love the fact that half portions of steak and delicious desserts are offered, and we have rarely been so impressed by a wine list (by both glass and bottle). Truly excellent. (☏010-290 94 54; www.ceobaasvanhetvlees.nl; Sumatraweg 1-3; mains €21-39; ⏱5-11pm Tue-Sat; Ⓜ Rijnhaven)

HMB
INTERNATIONAL €€

10 🍴 MAP P86, C2

Nestled in the shadow of the mighty Erasmusbrug, this sleek restaurant on the ground floor of the iconic De Rotterdam

(p88) building serves artistically presented contemporary cuisine. There's a strong international wine list, and service is attentive but unobtrusive. Check the website for full opening hours, as the restaurant closes for holidays a number of times each year. (☏010-760 06 20; www.hmb-restaurant.nl; Holland Amerika Kade 104; small plates €5-16, large plates €15-28, 3-course lunch menu €37.50, 4-/5-/6-course dinner menu €60/70/80; ⏱noon-3pm & 5.30-10pm Tue-Fri, 5.30-10pm Sat; ❄; Ⓜ Wilhelminaplein)

Posse
MEDITERRANEAN €€

11 🍴 MAP P86, B5

This place ticks every hipster box: set in a shabby but atmospheric warehouse next to the Fenix Food Factory, it has a vintage fitout, includes vegetarian and vegan options on its menu, hosts DJs spinning vinyl from its own collection, prioritises coffee and beer over wine and even supports group

Dining on Deliplein

Once home to the largest red-light district in Europe, Katendrecht is now one of Rotterdam's culinary hotspots. Deliplein is a small plaza right behind the Fenix Food Factory that houses more than 20 restaurants and bars, including upmarket steakhouse CEO Baas van Het Vlees (p91) and bohemian bar Café De Ouwehoer. Theater Walhalla (p94) on the plaza's western edge sometimes stages performances in the middle of the square.

bike rides. Living a cliché has never been so enjoyable. (☏010-737 18 15; www.posse.nl; Veerlaan 19a; mains €17-25; ☺noon-8.45pm Mon, Thu & Fri, 11am-8.45pm Sat, 11am-6pm Sun; Ⓜ Rijnhaven)

Kaapse Kitchen INTERNATIONAL €

Located in the Fenix Food Factory (p90), this open kitchen (see 8 ⓧ Map p86, B5) is operated by the Kaapse Brouwers brewery (p92). Each week, a different chef serves up global dishes made with local, organic and sustainable produce. (www.kaapsebrouwers.nl; Veerlaan 19d; prices vary; ☺4-10pm Mon-Fri, from noon Sat & Sun; Ⓜ Rijnhaven)

Rolph's Deli CAFE €

12 ⓧ MAP P86, C3

A haven off the wind tunnel that is Otto Reuchlinweg, this friendly deli offers all-day breakfasts and lunch options including salads and sandwiches. The 'all-in breakfast' (€12) is generous, tasty and great value. There are also plenty of fresh juices and smoothies on offer. (☏010 760 50 30; www.rolphsdeli.nl; Otto Reuchlinweg 974; breakfast dishes €5-12, sandwiches €6-24; ☺8am-4pm Mon-Fri, from 9am Sat, from 10am Sun; Ⓜ Wilhelminaplein)

Drinking

Kaapse Brouwers BREWERY

Beloved for its live-jazz nights on Fridays from 8pm, this craft brewery (see 8 ⓧ Map p86, B5) in the Fenix Food Factory (p90) brews a bitter, ale, IPAs and stout. Its onsite Kaapse Kitchen offers meals. There's indoor and outdoor seating. (☏010-218 08 53; www.kaapsebrouwers.nl; Veerlaan 19d; ☺noon-11pm Tue-Sun; Ⓜ Rijnhaven)

Café De Ouwehoer BAR

13 ⓟ MAP P86, B6

Offering plenty of the cosiness that the Dutch so prize, this atmospheric pub in the heart of Rotterdam's former harbour red-light district has an excellent selection of beers and whiskys and hosts occasional live-music acts. (☏010-486 52 53; Delistraat 36c;

⊗4pm-1am Mon-Thu, noon-2am Fri & Sat, noon-1am Sun; Ⓜ Rijnhaven)

Hotel NY Terrace Bar BAR

14 📍 MAP P86, B4

A truly marvellous location on the western point of Wilhelminapier, the terrace bar/cafe at Hotel New York (p91) offers a casual vibe and marvellous views of the Maas. In wet or windy weather, drinkers head to inside to the hotel's bar (7am to 1am). (📞010 439 05 25; https://hotel newyork.com/food-beverage/terrace/; Koninginnenhoofd 1; ⊗11am-midnight Apr-Nov; Ⓜ Wilhelminaplein)

nhow Bar COCKTAIL BAR

15 📍 MAP P86, C2

If Rotterdam had a 'best view from a cocktail bar' award, this bar on the 7th floor of the De Rotterdam building would be the clear winner. Action unfolds around the artfully illuminated bar or on the terrace with its spectacular view of the Erasmus-brug, and heats up on Friday and Saturday nights after 10pm, when a DJ coaxes the crowd into party mode. (📞010 206 76 00; www.nhow-rotterdam.com/ bar-kitchen; Wilhelminakade 137; ⊗7am-1am Sun-Thu, to 2am Fri & Sat; Ⓜ Wilhelminaplein)

Maassilo CLUB

16 📍 MAP P86, F8

With exposed pipes, graffiti-scrawled concrete pillars and metal railings, this former grain store from the early 20th century

Hotel New York (p91)

is now Rotterdam's biggest club. Depending on the night, expect DJs to pump out everything from thumping tech-house to bass-heavy Soca music. Check the online agenda for event details. (📞010-476 24 52; www.maassilo.com; Maashaven Zuidzijde 1-2; ⏰hrs vary; Ⓜ Maashaven)

Entertainment

Theater Walhalla
CABARET

17 ⭐ MAP P86, B6

Named after a shady pre-WWII dance hall that once entertained sailors in this area, this small theatre stages cabaret, music and theatre performances. On Sundays, there are often special shows for children. Check the website for program details. Card pay-

ments only. (📞010-215 22 76; www. theaterwalhalla.nl; Sumatraweg 9-11; ⏰performances Wed & Sun evenings, 1pm Sun; 👪; Ⓜ Rijnhaven)

LantarenVenster
CINEMA

18 ⭐ MAP P86, C4

Great art-house cinema with a convivial bar and cafe. (📞010-277 22 77; www.lantarenvenster.nl; Otto Reuchlinweg 996; adult/student €9.50/8; ⏰11.30am-1am Mon-Thu, 11.30am-2am Fri & Sat, 10am-midnight Sun; Ⓜ Wilhelminaplein)

Shopping

Booij Kaasmakers
FOOD

Making delicious cheeses for close on four centuries, this family business (see 8 ❌ Map p86,

Maassilo (p93)

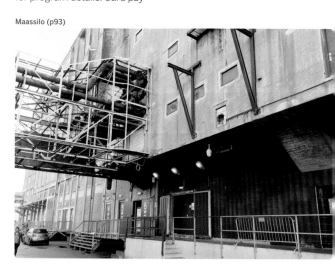

85) specialises in *buurenkaas* (neighbourhood cheese), which it makes on a farm outside Rotterdam. The company's wonderfully pungent store in the Fenix Food Factory (p90) sells its own produce as well as Spanish, Italian, French, Danish and Belgian varieties. It also sells eggs, milk and yoghurt. (☏010-418 53 10; www.booijkaasmakers.nl; Veerlaan 19d; MRijnhaven)

Tattoo Bob ART

19 🔒 MAP P86, B6

Tattoo Bob is a Rotterdam – and Katendrecht – legend, tattooing here on the cape since 1968. His children have since joined him in

Gay & Lesbian Film Festival

In summer, the Lantaren-Venster arthouse cinema (p94) presents its popular **Gay & Lesbian Summer Film Festival**, with films shown every Tuesday night. At this time, the cinema's bar becomes a popular meeting place for the local LGBTI community.

the business. You can have piercings done in this bright and spacious shop as well. (☏010-484 46 94; www.tattoobob.nl; Delistraat 4-10; ⏰1-10pm Mon-Sat; MRijnhaven)

South Holland Regions

Escher in Het Paleis

Mauritshuis

Den Haag (p113)
Cultural pursuits are a passion here, and sights such as world-famous Mauritshuis are sources of great local pride, as is the city's burgeoning foodie scene.

Delft (p99)
Preserved in all of its Golden Age glory, this compact and welcoming university town is known for its historic churches and world-famous pottery workshops.

Vermeer Centrum Delft

Explore
South Holland

Home to two of the country's major cities – Rotterdam and Den Haag – and to many of its prettiest and most historic towns, the province of Zuid-Holland (South Holland) is popular with domestic and international tourists alike. Known for its architecture, museums and sandy beaches, it is a region that richly rewards those who visit.

HVGO GROTIVS

Explore ◉
Delft

An amalgam of austere medieval magnificence and Golden Age glory, Delft's exquisite town centre is a hugely popular Dutch day-trip destination, awash with visitors strolling its narrow, canal-lined streets and picturesque central Markt. The centre is a true time capsule, having changed little since its most-famous resident, artist Johannes Vermeer, lived and worked here in the 17th century.

It pays to devote a full day to exploring the town. Start at the Museum Prinsenhof Delft (p105) and then move on to the Oude Kerk (p104) and Nieuwe Kerk (p104) before pausing for lunch at Kek (p107). In the afternoon, visit Vermeer Centrum (p100) and consider taking a factory tour at Royal Delft (p105) or De Delftse Pauw (p105). As the day draws to a close, take a walk around the Markt (p105), enjoy a drink at De Oude Jan (p109) or Café-Brasserie Belvédère (p110) and then adjourn to De Waag (p108) to enjoy dinner in its historic surrounds.

Getting There & Around

🚆 Frequent services from Rotterdam (€3.40, 15 minutes), Amsterdam (€13.20-15.60, one hour) and Den Haag (€2.50, 15 minutes).

🚋 Frequent services to/from Den Haag (€3.50, 15 minutes).

City Map on p102

Markt (p105) FRANK CORNELISSEN/SHUTTERSTOCK ©

Top Sights 📷
Vermeer Centrum Delft

The great painter Johannes Vermeer was born in Delft in 1632 and lived here until his death in 1675. Sadly, none of his works remain in the town. Going some way towards filling this gap is this tourist attraction, where reproductions of Vermeer's works are exhibited, a short film about his life is screened and displays about 17th-century painting techniques and materials give context.

◎ MAP P102, E3

📞 015-213 85 88

www.vermeerdelft.nl

Voldersgracht 21

adult/student/child 12-17 €9/7/5

🕙 10am-5pm

Downstairs

Housed in the historic site of the former St Lucas Guild, where Vermeer was Dean of Painters for many years, the centre is a great place to learn about the great man's life and work. Start by watching the short video presentation about his life (multiple languages available through audiophones) and then wander past 37 actual-size reproductions of his paintings arranged in chronological order. The authorship of a few of these has been questioned by some experts – see if you can spot why!

Upstairs

Afterwards, head upstairs to the centre's most interesting exhibits – a display on the pigments and tools that Vermeer would have used during his all-too-short working life and an interactive display on how he used light and shadow in his work – he is called 'the master of light' for good reason.

Conservation Video

Also upstairs is an interesting video presentation in which a conservator of painting discusses the 2010 restoration of Vermeer's *Woman in Blue Reading a Letter* (1663–64), part of the collection of the Rijksmuseum in Amsterdam. The painstaking restoration was funded with revenue gained by sending the painting to feature in a various exhibitions in galleries around the world. During the restoration, yellow varnish covering the work was removed and the Rijksmuseum's conservators were able to ascertain how Vermeer produced such an intense blue colour – he used a copper-green undercoat to give his blue extra depth.

★ **Top Tips**

o After viewing the reproductions here, head to the Mauritshuis (p114) in Den Haag and the Rijksmuseum in Amsterdam to see some of the originals.

o Free English-language guided tours of the museum are offered at 10.30am on Sundays.

o Be sure to take advantage of the free audioguide.

✕ **Take a Break**

After your visit, head to nearby Kek (p107) to enjoy an all-day breakfast, lunch, fresh juice or coffee.

Vermeer may well have visited De Waag (p108) when it functioned as a weigh house; now you can come here to enjoy a drink, light lunch or upmarket dinner.

DOELENPLEIN

A · B · C · D

1

5

Oude Delft

Voorstr

Verwersd

12

Dertienhuizen

2

Oude Kerkstr

Choorstr

Oude Kerk 2

De Vl

3

3

Museum Prinsenhof Delft

Heilige Geestkerkhof

16

Hippolytusbuurt

Papenstr

Volde

St Agathaplein

4

Nieuwstr

Markt

DELFT

8

Stadhu

11

5

Phoenixstr

Canal Boat Tour

Peperstr

Koornmark

6

Delft (1km)

Museum 7
Paul Tetar van Elven

A · B · C · D

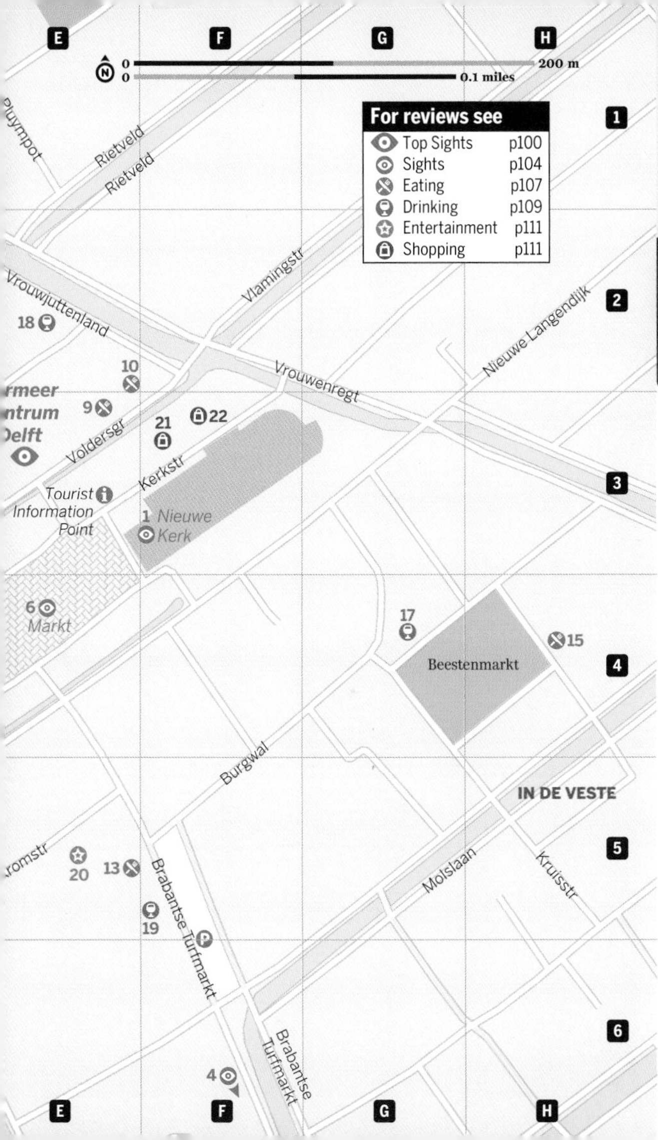

N

0 —————————— 200 m
0 —————————— 0.1 miles

For reviews see	
⦿ Top Sights	p100
⦿ Sights	p104
✕ Eating	p107
☕ Drinking	p109
★ Entertainment	p111
🔒 Shopping	p111

Pluympot

Rietveld

Rietveld

Vrouwjuttenland

18 ☕

Vlamingstr

Nieuwe Langendijk

Vrouwenregt

meer ntrum Delft ⦿

10 ✕

9 ✕

Voldersgr

21 🔒

🔒 22

Kerkstr

Tourist Information Point ℹ️

1 Nieuwe Kerk ⦿

6 ⦿ Markt

17 ☕

✕ 15

Beestenmarkt

Burgwal

IN DE VESTE

Kromstr

★ 20

13 ✕

Brabantse Turfmarkt

☕ 19

Molslaan

Kruisstr

🅿️

Brabantse Turfmarkt

4 ⦿

Sights

Nieuwe Kerk

CHURCH

1 ◎ MAP P102, F3

Construction of Delft's Nieuwe Kerk began in 1381; it was finally completed in 1655. The church has been the final resting place of almost every member of the House of Orange royal family since 1584, including William of Orange (William the Silent), who lies in an over-the-top marble mausoleum designed by Hendrick de Keyser. Children under five are not permitted to climb the 109m-high tower, whose 376 narrow, spiralling steps lead to panoramic views. (New Church; ☏ 015-212 30 25; https://oudeennieuwekerkdelft.nl/; Markt 80; adult/child 6-11 incl Oude Kerk €5/1,

Nieuwe Kerk tower additional €4/2; ⏰ 9am-6pm Mon-Sat Apr-Oct, 11am-4pm Mon-Fri, 10am-5pm Sat Nov-Jan, 10am-5pm Mon-Sat Feb & Mar)

Oude Kerk

CHURCH

2 ◎ MAP P102, B3

Founded c1246, the Oude Kerk is a surreal sight: its 75m-high tower, which was erected c1350, leans nearly 2m from the vertical due to subsidence caused by its canal location, hence its nickname Scheve Jan ('Leaning John'). The older section features an austere barrel vault; the newer northern transept has a Gothic vaulted ceiling. One of the tombs inside the church is that of painter Johannes Vermeer (p106). (Old Church; ☏ 015-212 30 15; https://oudeennieuwekerkdelft.nl/; Heilige Geestkerkhof 25; adult/child

Museum Prinsenhof Delft

5-11 incl Nieuwe Kerk €5/1; ⏰9am-5pm Mon-Sat Apr-Oct, 11am-4pm Mon-Fri, 10am-5pm Sat Nov-Jan, 10am-5pm Mon-Sat Feb & Mar)

Museum Prinsenhof Delft
MUSEUM

3 MAP P102, A3

William of Orange (William the Silent) was assassinated in this former convent in 1584 (the bullet hole in the wall is preserved), becoming the world's first political leader to be murdered by a handgun. Now a labyrinthine museum, it includes a room about the history of the House of Orange, an exhibit about Delft and innovation, and a dedicated exhibit titled 'Delftware: The Making of a Global Brand'. An audiotour of the building costs €1. (📞015-260 23 58; http://prinsenhof-delft.nl; St Agathaplein 1; adult/child 13-18/child 4-12 €12/6/3; ⏰11am-5pm Apr-Aug, closed Mon Sep-Mar)

Royal Delft
FACTORY

4 MAP P102, F6

Pottery fans will love visiting Royal Delft, the town's most famous Delftware (p111) factory. The admission ticket includes an audio tour that leads you through a painting demonstration, the company museum and the factory's production process. For many, of course, the tour highlight is the final stop in the gift shop. (Koninklijke Porceleyne Fles; 📞015-760 08 00; www.royaldelft.com; Rotterdamseweg 196; adult/child 13-18/child under 13

Exploring Delft by Boat

To float through Delft's canal-scapes, hop aboard the 45-minute **boat tour** (Map p102, D5; www.rondvaartdelft.nl; adult/child €8.50/4; ⏰hourly 11am-4pm Apr-Oct) operated by Rondvaartdelft. It departs from Koornmarkt 113, near Museum Paul Tetar van Elven.

€13.50/8.50/free; ⏰9am-5pm Mar-Oct, 9am-5pm Mon-Sat, noon-5pm Sun Nov-Feb)

De Delftse Pauw
FACTORY

5 MAP P102, A1

This long-operating Delftware (p111) factory north of the city centre offers free, short guided tours in which the production process is explained. These start every 10 minutes, and guides speak a number of languages. There are also weekday workshops in which you can paint a tile (€35) – advance bookings essential. Take tram 1 or 19 to Brasserskade. (The Delft Peacock; 📞015-212 49 20; www.delftpottery.com; Delftweg 133, Rijswijk; admission free; ⏰9am-4.30pm mid-Mar–Oct, 9am-4.30pm Mon-Fri, 11am-1pm Sat & Sun Nov–mid-Mar)

Markt
SQUARE

6 MAP P102, E4

One of the largest historic market squares in Europe, the rectangular

Vermeer: Delft's Most Famous Son

Johannes Vermeer (1632–75), one of the greatest of the Dutch Masters, lived his entire life in Delft, fathering 11 children and leaving behind fewer than 40 paintings. (The actual number is disputed as the authorship of some canvasses attributed to him has been called into question by modern-day Vermeer experts.) Vermeer's works have rich and meticulous colouring and he captured light as few other painters have ever managed to do. His subjects were drawn from everyday life in Delft, his interiors depicting domestic scenes, and his portraits – the most famous of which is the *Girl with a Pearl Earring* (1665) – were both fond and remarkably lifelike.

Vermeer's best-known exterior work, *View of Delft* (c 1660–61) brilliantly captures the play of light and shadow of a partly cloudy day. It's possible to visit the location where he painted it, across the canal at Hooikade, southeast of the train station. Unfortunately, none of Vermeer's works remain in Delft, although the Vermeer Centrum Delft (p100) gives a good introduction to his life and work, and the tourist office (p147) sells a 'Vermeer Trail' walking tour brochure (€2.50). Both *Girl with a Pearl Earring* and *View of Delft* can be seen at the Mauritshuis (p114) in Den Haag, while arguably his most famous painting, *The Milkmaid*, resides in Amsterdam's Rijksmuseum alongside *Woman in Blue Reading a Letter* (1663–64), amongst other works.

Vermeer's life is something of an enigma, but his fame as a painter has long been acknowledged. The 2003 film *Girl with a Pearl Earring* (based on Tracy Chevalier's novel) speculated on his relationship with the eponymous girl. The following year, a work long thought to be a forgery was finally confirmed as authentic – *Young Woman Seated at the Virginals* was the first Vermeer to be auctioned in more than 80 years, selling to an anonymous buyer for €24 million.

The excellent website www.essentialvermeer.com has exhaustive details on the painter and his works, including where his paintings are exhibited at any given time.

Markt was first paved in the late 15th century. It is edged by Stadhuis (p107), Nieuwe Kerk (p104), cafes, boutiques and souvenir shops. A market is held here on Thursdays.

Museum Paul Tetar van Elven

MUSEUM

7 ◎ MAP P102, D6

Off the usual tourist radar, this museum is the former studio and home of 19th-century Dutch artist Paul Tetar van Elven, who lived and worked here from 1864 until 1894, and bequeathed it to the town. The museum features his reproductions of notable paintings (this was his speciality), along with antique furniture, oriental porcelain and Delftware that he collected. The evocative interior retains its original furnishings and lived-in feel. (☏015-212 42 06; www.tetar.nl; Koornmarkt 67; adult/student & child €5/free; ⏱1-5pm Tue-Sun)

Stadhuis HISTORIC BUILDING

8 ◉ MAP P102, D4

Delft's town hall has an unusual combination of Renaissance construction surrounding an early 14th-century tower. (Town Hall; Markt)

Eating

Kek CAFE €

9 ✖ MAP P102, E3

The baskets of organic fruit and vegetables at the front of this stylish cafe are a good indicator of what's on the menu – freshly squeezed juices, fruit smoothies and a tempting array of cakes, muffins, tarts and sandwiches made with local seasonal produce (no-sugar, vegan and gluten-free options available). Other draws include all-day breakfasts and coffee made using Giraffe beans, roasted in Rotterdam. (☏015-750 32 53; http://kekdelft.nl/; Voldersgracht 27; breakfast dishes €4-10, sandwiches €6-10; ⏱8.30am-6pm; 🛜🌱)

Stadhuis

Puro Cucina

CAFE €

10 MAP P102, E2

Describing itself as a cooking studio, this hybrid cafe and cooking school has a sleek modern interior arranged around an open kitchen. The menu offers breakfast favourites (pancakes with ricotta and honey, granola with yoghurt and fruit), simple but tasty lunch dishes (pasta dish of the day, salads) and homemade cake with coffee at all times of the day. (📞015-820 03 90; www.purocucina.nl; Voldersgracht 28; breakfast dishes €6-10, lunch dishes €5-14; ⏰9am-6pm Wed-Mon)

De Waag

CAFE €€

11 MAP P102, D4

With a sprawling terrace behind the Stadhuis and atmospheric eating and drinking spaces inside this 16th-century *waag* (weighing house), this is a perfect spot for a post-sightseeing beer. The food is quite good, too – enjoy one of the globally inspired dishes in the upmarket restaurant on the first floor (dinner only) or opt for a more casual meal downstairs. (📞015-213 03 93; www.de-waag.nl; Markt 11; sandwiches €4-10, cafe mains €15-20, restaurant mains €24; ⏰kitchen 11am-10pm Sun & Mon, 10am-10pm Tue-Sat; 🛜📶)

La Fontanella

ITALIAN €€

12 MAP P102, D1

The ultimate Italian neighbourhood restaurant, La Fontanella has been at this location since 1974. It imports its ingredients from Italy and offers a well-priced menu of an antipasto and a pizza or pasta main for €13. (📞015-212 58 74; www.fontanella.nl; Verwersdijk 30; pizza & pasta €7-11.50, mains €18-24; ⏰5-10pm Tue-Sun)

IJs Van Jans

ICE CREAM

13 MAP P102, E5

Enjoying a cone or cup of the artisanal ice cream and sorbet sold at this parlour is a popular pastime when promenading through the town centre. The rich chocolate, salted caramel and yoghurt, honey and walnut flavours are particularly *lekker* (yummy). (📞015-820 09 70; www.jansdelft.nl/ijs; Brabantse Turfmarkt 87; per scoop €1.25; ⏰10am-5.30pm Mon & Sun, 9am-5.30pm Tue-Fri, 8.30am-5.30pm Sat, reduced hrs winter; 📶)

Beestenmarkt Plaza

As the name suggests, Beestenmarkt (Animal Market) once the site of the town's cattle market. This large open space is filled with plane trees and surrounded by fine buildings now housing an array of popular bars and restaurants. All have outdoor tables that fill quickly on summer evenings. Our favourite is Café-Brasserie Belvédère (p110).

Brasserie 't Crabbetje

SEAFOOD €€

4 MAP P102, D1

Seafood is given the gourmet treatment at this unassuming restaurant – everything from scallops to lobster, sea bass to king crab. (☑015-213 88 50; www.crabbetjedelft.nl; Verwersdijk 14; mains €19-36, 3-course tasting menu €36.50; ☺5.30-10pm Wed-Sun; ☎)

Spijshuis de Dis

DUTCH €€

5 MAP P102, H4

Fresh fish and soups served in bread bowls take centre stage at this old-fashioned option, but meat eaters and vegetarians are catered for too. In summer, the outdoor tables here and at the many other restaurants on the

Beestenmarkt are lovely spots to enjoy dinner. (☑015-213 17 82; www.spijshuisdedis.com; Beestenmarkt 36; mains €17-25; ☺5-10pm Tue-Sat; ☎)

Drinking

De Oude Jan

BROWN CAFE

16 MAP P102, B3

Opposite the Oude Kerk, this is one of Delft's most popular hangouts. It's known for student-friendly hours and occasional performances by live bands, who take to the umbrella-shaded courtyard's outdoor stage (the timber-lined cafe interior is far too small). Food is served during the day (toasties €3 to €4, burgers €13). (☑015-214 53 63; www.oudejan.nl; Heilige Geestkerkhof 4; ☺10am-1am Mon, to 4am Tue-Thu & Sun, to

Kek (p107)

Delftware at Royal Delft (p105)

3am Fri & Sat Easter-Oct, from noon Nov-Easter; 🛜)

Café-Brasserie Belvédère

BEER GARDEN

17 🍴 MAP P102, G4

Belgian beer is the popular choice here, enjoyed in great quantities at a sea of tables in leafy Beestenmarkt (p108). There are more than 10 beers on tap, and pub-style grub including mussels. (📞015-212 32 97; www.bbcbelvedere. nl; Beestenmarkt 8; ⏰11am-1am Mon-Thu, 11am-2am Fri, 10am-2am Sat, noon-1am Sun)

Doerak

PUB

18 🍴 MAP P102, E2

Canal-side and pavement seating are popular perches at this friendly drinking den, but regulars tend to claim seats at the long indoor bar before ordering their tipples from a huge array of craft and Trappist beers, 12 of which are on tap. (📞06 4569 4928; www.cafedoerak. nl; Vrouwjuttenland 17; ⏰3pm-1am Mon-Thu, 3pm-2am Fri, noon-2am Sat, 1pm-1am Sun)

Locus Publicus

BROWN CAFE

19 🍴 MAP P102, F5

Cosy little Locus Publicus is filled with cheery locals quaffing their way through the 200-strong beer list, including 13 on tap. There's great people-watching from the front terrace. (📞015-213 46 32; www.facebook.com/locuspublicus delft/; Brabantse Turfmarkt 67; ⏰11am-1am Mon-Thu, to 2am Fri & Sat, noon-1am Sun; 🛜)

Famous Delftware

Delft's eponymous blue-and-white china is ubiquitous throughout town. Given that the process was first developed in China, it's ironic that the mass of fake Delftware now sold in the tourist shops around town also comes from that part of the world.

The real stuff is produced in fairly small quantities at a few factories in and around Delft. To purchase some to take home, visit Royal Delft (p105), De Delftse Pauw (p105), De Candelaer or De Blauwe Tulp.

Entertainment

Bebop Jazzcafé   LIVE MUSIC

20 ⭐ MAP P102, E5

Live jazz plays every Sunday at this *bruin café* (traditional Dutch pub), which has a dark indoor space and a summer-only beer garden. There are jam sessions on Tuesdays, live bebop on Wednesdays and jazz on some Sunday afternoons. Check the Facebook feed for the program. (☎015-213 52 10; www.facebook.com/Jazzcafe Bebop/; Kromstraat 33; ⊙8pm-1am Mon, 4pm-1am Tue-Thu & Sun, 4pm-2am Fri, 3pm-2am Sat)

Shopping

De Blauwe Tulp   CERAMICS

21 🏠 MAP P102, F3

Delftware is painted and sold in this studio and shop near the Markt. (☎015-214 80 92; www.bluetulip.nl; Kerkstraat 12; ⊙9.30am-5.30pm Mon-Sat)

De Candelaer   CERAMICS

22 🏠 MAP P102, F3

Delftware outfit De Candelaer is located just off the Markt. It employs three artists, who don't seem to mind customers watching them while they work. (☎015-213 18 48; www.candelaer.nl; Kerkstraat 13a; ⊙9.30am-5.30pm Mon-Fri, to 5pm Sat May-Sep, shorter hrs Oct-Mar)

Explore ◈
Den Haag

There's a lot more to Den Haag (The Hague) than immediately meets the eye. The popular perception of the Netherlands' third-largest city is of a stately, regal place populated with bureaucrats and businesspeople. While this is true to some extent, there is so much more: most notably the city's rich cultural and culinary scenes.

If you've only got one day to explore, you'll need to identify two or three city highlights to anchor your itinerary. Most are in or close to the city centre, so can be visited on foot or by tram. Prioritise the Maurits- huis (p114), which deserves at least three hours, and then decide between Escher in Het Paleis (p116), the Gemeentemuseum (p122) or the Panorama Mesdag (p122). In between, enjoy lunch somewhere on Denne- weg, browse the boutiques around Noordeinde, dine at elegant Fouquet (p127) and then party the night away at the Grote Markt bars and at legendary live-music venue, Paard (p133).

Getting There & Around

🚆 Frequent services from Rotterdam (€4.70, 19 to 30 minutes) and Delft (€2.50, 7 to 16 minutes) to Den Haag Centraal Station (CS) or Den Haag Hollands Spoor (HS).

Ⓜ Metro line E links Rotterdam's city centre with Den Haag's Centraal Station (€4.90, 30 minutes).

🚊 The best way to get around the city; most routes converge on Centraal Station. One-hour tickets cost €3.50 and can be purchased on board lines 1, 6, 12 and 16.

City Map on p120

Top Sights 📷
Mauritshuis

One of the world's great art museums, the Mauritshuis (set in a 17th-century mansion built for wealthy sugar trader Johan Maurits) is the repository of masterpieces of the Dutch Golden Age. The collection numbers more than 200 works, and includes paintings by anyone who was anyone in the 17th-century Dutch and Flemish art worlds – Vermeer, Rembrandt, Rubens, Hals and many others are all well represented.

◎ MAP P120, D5

☎ 070-302 34 56

www.mauritshuis.nl

Plein 29

adult/student/child under 19 €15.50/12.50/free

🕑 1-6pm Mon, 10am-6pm Tue, Wed & Fri-Sun, 10am-8pm Thu

🚊 Centrum

The Art of Portraiture

The museum's collection is rich in portraits, and one of the most charming is the richly coloured *Portrait of Elisabeth Bellinghausen* (1538–39) by German painter Bartholomäus Bryn I. Find it in room seven.

Local Scenes

One of the museum's most recognisable works is *Ice Scene* (c 1610) by Amsterdam-born artist Hendrick Avercamp. This depicts skaters having fun on a frozen river, with windmills and thatched houses shown in the background. You'll find it in room eight.

The Big Guns

The museum's second-floor galleries are home to significant works by Dutch Golden Age masters Frans Hals, Johannes Vermeer and Rembrandt (no surname necessary). In room nine, look out for Hals' lovely portraits of Aletta Hanemans (1625) and her husband Jacob Olycan (1625) before turning your attention to the museum's cache of works by Rembrandt. These include the huge and gruesome *The Anatomy Lesson of Dr Nicolaes Tulp* (1632), painted in Amsterdam when he was only 25, as well as his famous naked *Susanna* (1636). More Rembrandts can be found in the next room.

The Jewel of the Collection

There are many wonderful works in the Mauritshuis, but one stands above all the others for its charm and fame. Vermeer's *Girl with a Pearl Earring* (c 1665) is the pride of the museum's collection, used on almost all of its marketing material and beloved by all who see it. Find it in room 15, alongside Vermeer's *View of Delft* (c 1660–61) with its wonderful interplay of light and shade.

★ Top Tips

○ Visit the museum's gift shop to source postcards, books and tasteful souvenirs to take home.

○ Download a free multimedia smart tour of the museum at the Apple Store or on Google Play.

○ Your ticket includes entry to nearby Galerij Prins Willem V (p124).

✕ Take a Break

The museum's brasserie (p130) serves soup, sandwiches and salads for lunch and a selection of *borrel hapjes* (snacks) to enjoy with an afternoon beer or glass of wine.

Nearby De Basiliek (p127) serves excellent Mediterranean cuisine and is a great choice for lunch or dinner

Top Sights 📷
Escher in Het Paleis

Celebrating the work of Dutch graphic artist MC Escher (1898–1972), this museum in the 18th-century Lange Voorhout Palace displays 150 of his woodcuts and lithographs, including many of his best-known works. Fascinated by mathematical patterns, Escher investigated themes of repetition, circularity, infinity and symmetry throughout his unique career.

◎ MAP P120, D3

📞 070-427 77 30

www.escherinhetpaleis.nl

Lange Voorhout 74

adult/student/child 7-15/child under 7 €10/8.50/6.50/free

🕐 11am-5pm Tue-Sun

🚋 Korte Voorhout

Lange Voorhout Palace

Dating from 1760, the building housing the museum was purchased in 1896 by Queen Emma, great-great grandmother of the current king (Willem-Alexander), who used it as a winter residence until her death in 1934. The museum moved into the building in 2002, perhaps attracted by its beautiful staircase, which appears to go up to the second floor but doesn't – a very Escher-like optical illusion.

Early Works

The former rear drawing room on the ground floor now houses a number of Escher's early works, including woodcuts inspired by trips to Italy. His *Inside St Peter's, Rome* (1934) displays the unorthodox use of perspective that was to become one of his trademarks. Also in this room is the well-known *Tower of Babel* (1928), another experiment with perspective.

The Metamorphoses

A circular work inspired by Escher's preoccupation with the interlinked concepts of eternity and infinity, *Metamorphosis III* (1967–68) evokes time and space running parallel in an unending circle. His largest-ever print, the 7m-long work was printed on 33 blocks on six combined sheets before being partly coloured by hand and mounted on canvas. Its imagery includes an Italian city, a chess game, bees, fish, birds, horses and boats. In the same room, two other *Metamorphosis* works (*I* and *II*) show a similar preoccupation with the theme of the cycle.

★ **Top Tips**

○ Combination tickets to this museum and either Madurodam (p124), Panorama Mesdag (p122) or Gemeentemuseum (p122) will result in savings and are available at the ticket office.

○ It pays to do some background research on Escher and his art before visiting, as labelling in the museum is limited.

✕ **Take a Break**

Pop into nearby luxury hotel **Hotel Des Indes** (Map p120, C3; ☏ 070-361 23 45; www.hoteldesindes thehague.com; Lange Voorhout 54-56; s/d/ste from €155/169/469; P ❄ 🛜) to enjoy a lavish high tea between 2pm and 3.30pm (€39 weekdays, €41 weekends).

Just north of the museum, Denneweg (p128) is one of the city's major foodie strips, with cafes and restaurants galore.

Walking Tour

The Palace Precinct

Kings, queens and courtiers have lived and worked in the heart of Den Haag for centuries. This part of town has managed to retain its historic buildings and refined ambiance while embracing a exciting influx of hipster cafes, avant-garde boutiques and cutting-edge art galleries.

Walk Facts

Start Paleis Noordeinde
End Hofvijver
Length 2km; three hours

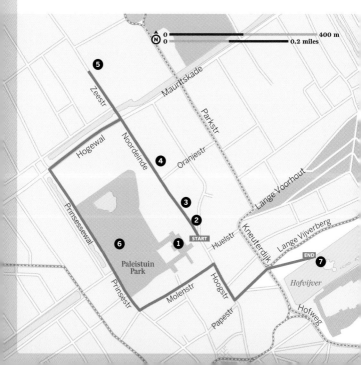

❶ Paleis Noordeinde

Begin your perambulation outside the Paleis Noordeinde (p126), a home of members of the family of Orange Nassau since 1595. Extensively rebuilt in the early 19th century, it now functions as King Willem-Alexander's workplace and state office. Admire the building's classical facade through the crested gate.

❷ Statue

Turn your attention to the 19th-century equestrian statue out front, which depicts William of Orange. This important figure in Dutch history led the Dutch revolt against the Spanish Habsburgs that set off the Eighty Years' War (1568–1648) and resulted in the formal independence of the United Provinces in 1581.

❸ Bookstor

From the statue, walk north up Noordeinde, one of the city's most interesting shopping and cafe strips. Pop into Bookstor (p135) to browse its shelves.

❹ Lola Bikes & Coffee

Continue to Lola Bikes & Coffee (p131), where you should stop for a well-made espresso and perhaps for some advice about what bike routes to follow around South Holland – these guys are the experts.

❺ Panorama Mesdag

Continue up the street, investigating shops that catch your eye before crossing the canal and visiting the Panorama Mesdag (p122), a small museum housing a 19th-century panoramic painting by Hendrik Willem Mesdag depicting the sea, sand dunes and fishing village of Scheveningen.

❻ Paleistuin Park

From here, backtrack to Hogewal, veer right (west) and follow the canal as far as Prinsessewal, where you turn left (south) and walk to the Paleistuin Park at the rear of the Paleis Noordeinde. It is known to locals as the 'Secret Garden'. Wander past its flowerbeds, fountains, hedgerows and ponds.

❼ Hofvijver

Continue to Molenstraat, another popular shopping and eating strip. At the junction of Noordeinde, veer right (south) and then left at Plaats, which will bring you to the Hofvijver (p126), a large ornamental pond which has the Binnenhof and Mauritshuis as a backdrop. Taking a few photographs from this ultra-Instagrammable location will mark the end of your walk and give you time to plan your next move.

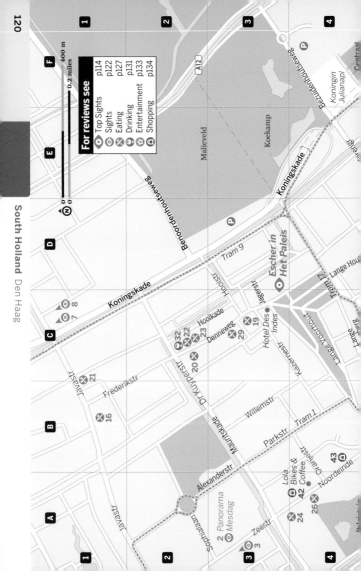

For reviews see

◎ Top Sights   p114
◉ Sights   p122
✖ Eating   p127
❸ Drinking   p131
❶ Entertainment   p133
🛍 Shopping   p134

400 m
0.2 miles

A12

Malieveld

Koekamp

Benoordenhoutseweg

Koningskade

Koningskade

Bezuidenhoutseweg

Koningin
Julianapl

Tram 9

Escher in
Het Paleis ◎

Hoornstr

Jagerstr

Tram 17

Lange Hou

Hooikade

Denneweg

Hotel Des
Indes ●

Kazernestr

Lange Voorhout

Lange

Frederikstr

Dr Kuyperstr

Javastr

Maurtiskade

Willemstr

Parkstr   Tram 1

Sophiaiaan

Alexanderstr

Panorama
Mesdag ◉

Zeestr

Lola
Bikes &
Coffee ●

Oranjestr

Noordeinde

Javastr

✖32
✖22
✖23
✖19
✖29
✖20
✖21
✖16
✖24
✖26
◎7
◎8
◎3
🅿
🅿
2
42
43

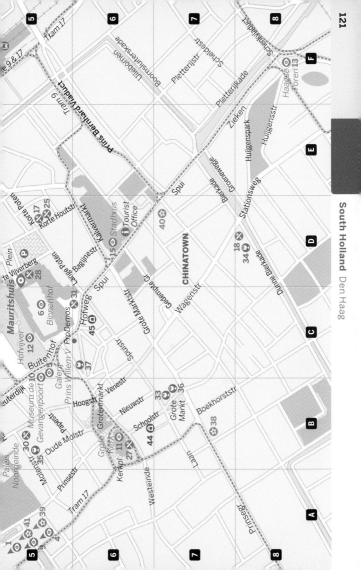

Sights

Gemeentemuseum

MUSEUM

1 ⊙ MAP P120, A5

Known predominantly for its De Stijl exhibit, this museum is housed in an unusual art deco building designed by HP Berlage. It opened in 1935. The De Stijl exhibit suffers from an overemphasis on unremarkable pre–De Stijl paintings by Piet Mondrian, but the major drawcard, his unfinished *Victory Boogie Woogie* (1942–44), is an undoubted masterpiece. Upstairs, the 'Discover the Modern' exhibit includes Egon Schiele's exquisite *Portrait of Edith* (1915) among early-20th-century works by Van Gogh, Picasso, Kandinsky and others. (Municipal Museum; ☏070-338 11 11; www.gemeentemuseum.nl; Stadhouderslaan 41; adult/child €15/free, combination ticket with Fotomuseum Den Haag & GEM €19/free; ⊙10am-5pm Tue-Sun; ☐Gemeentemuseum/Museon)

Panorama Mesdag

GALLERY

2 ⊙ MAP P120, A3

Home to the *Panorama* (1881), an immense, 14m-high, 360-degree painting of the sea, dunes and fishing village of Scheveningen, this museum is one of Den Haag's most unusual cultural attractions. The work, which is 120m in circumference, was created by Hendrik Willem Mesdag (1831–1915), a member of the Impressionist-influenced Hague School of painters. Viewed from an upper platform, it gives the illusion that the

Panorama Mesdag

Portrait of Edith

Part of the collection of the Gemeentemuseum (p122), this much-loved portrait of Edith Schiele was painted by her husband, Austrian artist Egon Schiele, in 1915. Wearing a striped, multicoloured dress that she had made from curtain fabric for her wedding to Schiele in that same year, Edith looks beautiful but timid – perhaps overwhelmed by the dramatic lead-up to her marriage day. (Schiele had previously been romantically involved with Edith's sister Adele, and her family were very much opposed to his relationship with Edith.)

Tragically, both Edith and Egon died within three years of this portrait being painted, victims of the Spanish Flu pandemic that swept Europe at that time. Edith was six month pregnant when she died on 28 October 1918; Egon died three days later.

viewer is high on a dune looking at the scene. (☎070-310 66 65; www.panorama-mesdag.com; Zeestraat 65; adult/student/child 4-11 €10/8.50/5; ☺10am-5pm Mon-Sat, 11am-5pm Sun; 🚋Mauritskade)

Vredespaleis
HISTORIC SITE

3 ◉ MAP P120, A3

Home to the UN's Permanent Court of Arbitration and International Court of Justice, the Peace Palace is housed in a grand 1913 building donated by American steelmaker Andrew Carnegie. Its **visitor centre** has multimedia exhibits detailing the history of both the building and the organisations within; these are enjoyed in a free 30-minute audioguide tour. Hour-long guided afternoon tours of the palace in Dutch and English are offered on weekends; these should be booked ahead on the website. (Peace Palace; ☎070-302 42 42; www.vredespaleis.nl; Carnegieplein 2; visitor centre admission free, tours adult/child under 9 €11/free; ☺visitor centre 10am-5pm Tue-Sun Apr-Oct, 11am-4pm Tue-Sun Nov-Mar; 🚋Vredespaleis)

Fotomuseum Den Haag
MUSEUM

4 ◉ MAP P120, A5

Adjoining the Gemeentemuseum (p122) and sharing a building with GEM (p124), Den Haag's excellent photography museum mounts several major exhibitions a year. The ground-floor cafe overlooks the ornamental lake in front of the Gemeentemuseum and is a popular meeting spot in this part of town. (☎070-338 11 44; www.fotomuseumdenhaag.nl; Stadhouderslaan 43; incl GEM entry adult/child €8/free, combination ticket with Gemeentemuseum €19/free; ☺11am-6pm Tue-Sun; 🚋Gemeentemuseum/Museon)

Galerij Prins Willem V GALLERY

5 ◉ MAP P120, C5

Sharing an entrance with the Gevangenpoort (p125), this was the first public museum in the Netherlands when it opened in 1774 as a showcase of William V's art collection. It closed after many of its works were 'acquired' by the occupying French in 1794 and didn't reopen in the same location until 2010. Today, the fully restored gallery houses 150 old masters from the Mauritshuis collection (Steen, Rubens, Potter et al) hung cheek-by-jowl in the style of the late 18th century. (www.mauritshuis.nl; Buitenhof 33; adult/child under 19 €5/free, combined ticket with Mauritshuis adult/child under 19 €15.50/free, combined ticket with Museum de Gevangenpoort adult/child under 13 €12.50/6; ◷noon-5pm Tue-Sun; 🚊 Kneuterdijk)

Binnenhof PALACE

6 ◉ MAP P120, C5

Home to both houses of the Dutch government, this complex of buildings next to the Hofvijver (p126) is arranged around a central courtyard that was once used for executions. Its splendid ceremonial **Ridderzaal** (Knights Hall) dates back to the 13th century. The 17th-century North Wing is still home to the Upper House, but the Lower House meets in a chamber in the modern eastern part of the complex. Visitor organisation **ProDemos** (Map p120, C6; ☏070-757 02 00; www.prodemos.nl; Hofweg 1; Ridderzaal tour €5.50, Ridderzaal, House

of Representatives & Senate tour €11; ◷office 10am-5pm Mon-Sat, tours by reservation; 🚊 Kneuterdijk, Centrum) conducts guided tours. (🚊 Centrum)

Madurodam AMUSEMENT PARK

7 ◉ MAP P120, C1

A miniaturised Netherlands, this theme park sports 1:25 scale versions of Schiphol, Amsterdam, windmills and tulips, Rotterdam harbour, the Delta dykes and more. It's an enlightening example of the Dutch tendency to put their world under a microscope. Kids love it. (☏070-416 24 00; www.madurodam.nl; George Maduroplein 1; weekday/weekend €16.50/17.50, family/child under 3 €52.50/free; ◷9am-8pm mid-Mar–Aug, 9am-7pm Sep & Oct, 11am-5pm Nov–mid-Mar; 👶; 🚊 Madurodam)

Scheveningen BEACH

8 ◉ MAP P120, C1

The long sandy beach at Scheveningen attracts nine million visitors per year. Though the water and sand are clean, the beach is heavily developed, with numerous cafes elbowing each other for space on tiers of beachside promenades. The beach is overlooked by the grand, 1818 Kurhaus, a hotel with a restaurant and bar (with outdoor terrace) that are open to the public. (🚊 Rtes 1 & 11)

GEM MUSEUM

9 ◉ MAP P120, A5

One of the contemporary wings of the neighbouring Gemeente-

Madurodam

museum (p122), this fine art museum shares a building with the Fotomuseum Den Haag (p123) and stages a constantly changing program of exhibitions by Dutch and international visual artists. You're as likely to see video installations as you are painting, sculpture, drawing, film and photography. (☏070-338 11 11; www.gem-online.nl; Stadhouderslaan 43; incl Fotomuseum Den Haag entry adult/child €8/free, combination ticket with Gemeentemuseum €19/free; ⏰11am-6pm Tue-Sun; 🚊Gemeentemuseum/Museon)

Museum de Gevangenpoort   MUSEUM

10 ◉ MAP P120, C5

A remnant of the 13th-century city fortifications, the Gevangen-

poort functioned as a prison from 1428 to 1825. Guided tours (30 minutes) run hourly on weekdays and every half-hour on weekends, evoking what life would have been like for both prisoners and their gaolers. Tours are not suitable for young children, as some guides take a ghoulish delight in describing the incarceration and torture of miscreants in vivid detail. English-language tours are offered at 2.15pm on Saturday and Sunday. (Museum the Prison Gate; ☏070-346 08 61; www.gevangenpoort.nl; Buitenhof 33; adult/child under 13 €10/6, combination ticket with Galerij Prins Willem V €12.50/6; ⏰10am-5pm Tue-Fri, from noon Sat & Sun, last tour 3.45pm; 🚊Kneuterdijk)

The Former Capital

Den Haag is the Dutch seat of government and home to the royal family. Prior to 1806, it was the Dutch capital; however, that year Louis Bonaparte installed his government in Amsterdam. Eight years later, when the French had been ousted, the government returned to Den Haag but the title of capital remained with Amsterdam.

Grote Kerk   CHURCH

11 ◉ MAP P120, B6

Dating from 1450, the Great Church has a fine pulpit that was constructed in the following century. If you're here outside its limited visitor season (note that opening hours can be unreliable), you can take in concerts and organ recitals – check its online agenda for dates. The neighbouring **Oude Raadhuis** (Old Town Hall; 1565) is a splendid example of Dutch Renaissance architecture. (☏070-302 86 30; www.grotekerkdenhaag.nl; Rond de Grote Kerk 12; adult/child under 12 €2/free; ☺11am-5pm Tue-Sat, 2-5pm Sun late May–Sep; ☒Grote Markt)

Hofvijver   POND

12 ◉ MAP P120, C5

Overlooked by both the Binnenhof (p124) and the Mauritshuis (p114), the picturesque Hofvijver pond inspires countless snapshots. (Court Pond; ☒Centrum)

Haagse Toren   VIEWPOINT

13 ◉ MAP P120, F8

A glass elevator whisks you up in just 40 seconds to the observation deck on the 42nd floor (135m) of this tower; there's also a less-dizzying option of riding a window-less lift. On a clear day, panoramas from the indoor viewing areas and outdoor balcony extend as far as Rotterdam, Leiden and Hoek van Holland. Tickets include a beer, house wine or soft drink in the Sky Bar (after 6pm this offer stretches to a cocktail). (☏070-305 10 00; www.haagsetoren.nl; Rijswijkseplein 786; admission €9; ☺observation deck noon-10pm; ☒Rijswijkseplein)

Paleis Noordeinde   PALACE

14 ◉ MAP P120, B5

The king's and queen's official quarters at Paleis Noordeinde is not open to the public. The Renaissance formality of the structure is fittingly regal, and the setting next to the Paleistuin Park (open to the public) is quite lovely. (Noordeinde; ☒Kneuterdijk)

Stadhuis   ARCHITECTURE

15 ◉ MAP P120, D6

Designed by US architect Richard Meier and completed in 1995, this often-maligned, huge, blindingly white building is usually referred to as the 'Ice Palace'. It houses the city administration, main municipal library, tourist information centre and public toilets (€0.30). (Town Hall; Spui 70; ☺7am-7pm Mon-

Wed & Fri, 7am-9.30pm Thu, 9.30am-5pm Sat; 🚊Kalvermarkt-Stadhuis)

Eating

Fouquet

DUTCH €€€

⑯ 🍴 MAP P120, B1

The three-course 'market fresh' menu at this elegant restaurant is an excellent and bargain-priced introduction to Sebastiaan de Bruijn's seasonally inspired French-Mediterranean fare. The menu changes daily, responding to what is fresh in the local markets, and is prepared with love and great expertise. Presentation, service and the wine list are all equally impressive. (📞070-360 62 73; www.fouquet.nl; Javastraat 31a; mains €25-28, 3-course menus €30-38; ⏱6-

9.30pm Mon-Sat; 🍴; 🚊Javastraat, Javabrug)

De Basiliek

INTERNATIONAL €€

⑰ 🍴 MAP P120, D5

Moody lighting, comfortable seating and unobtrusive service set the scene for enjoyable meals at this classy choice. The menu is predominantly Italian and French, with a few Indian and Middle Eastern dishes thrown in as wildcards. The food is fresh and full of flavour, made with top-notch produce, and the stellar wine includes loads of by-the-glass options. Great coffee too. (📞070-360 61 44; www.debasiliek.nl; Korte Houtstraat 4a; mains €18-24, 3-course menu €37.50-42.50; ⏱noon-4pm & 6-10pm Mon-Fri, 6-10pm Sat; 🛜🍴; 🚊Kalvermarkt-Stadhuis)

Paleis Noordeinde

Eat Street

One of the oldest streets in Den Haag, **Denneweg** has retained many of its 18th-century buildings. Until recent years, these were housing antiques shops. These days the street is full of cafes, bars and restaurants and has built the reputation as Den Haag's foodie hotspot. Notable eateries include Dekxels, Oker (p129), Oogst and Walter Benedict (p129).

Basaal
MEDITERRANEAN €€

18 🗺 MAP P120, D8

Neighbourhood bistros are rarely as stylish as this one, and few have locations as pretty. Overlooking a canal, with waterside seating in summer, it offers well-priced modern Mediterranean fare and a similarly focused wine list. Chef Bas Oonk uses regional seasonal produce to create meat and fish dishes bursting with flavour; his three-course Bib-Gourmand menu (€36.50) is a steal. (📞070-427 68 88; www.restaurantbasaal.nl; Dunne Bierkade 3; mains €21-24, set menus €37-60; ⏱6-10pm Tue-Sat; 🚊Bierkade)

Oogst
MEDITERRANEAN €€

19 🗺 MAP P120, C3

Classy is the appropriate descriptor for this small restaurant on Den Haag's prime foodie stretch, and it applies to everything from the interior (brocade-covered banquettes, fine napery, delicate glassware) to the food menu (small, beautifully presented plates). The chef uses super-fresh produce to create dishes that are both delicious and easy on the wallet. (📞070-360 92 24; www.restaurantoogst.nl; Denneweg 10b; small plates €9, 4-course small-plate menu €30; ⏱noon-2pm & 6-10pm Tue-Sat; 🖊; 🚊Malieveld, Dr Kuyperstraat)

Dekxels
INTERNATIONAL €€

20 🗺 MAP P120, C2

A member of Den Haag's ever-growing coterie of bistros with menus dominated by small plates rather than main courses, Dekxels concentrates on Asian dishes but also draws on Italy for inspiration. Flavours are good, though presentation is overly fussy. The well-priced wine list trawls the globe. (📞070-365 97 88; www.dekxels.nl; Denneweg 130; 4-course small-plate menu from €31.50; ⏱5.30-11pm; 🖊; 🚊Dr Kuyperstraat)

Raffles
INDONESIAN €€

21 🗺 MAP P120, C1

Specialising in satay, this up-market Indonesian restaurant focuses on classic dishes from Central Java but supplements these with choices from other Indonesian regions, Malaysia and Singapore. The food is good, although perhaps a tad bland for some palates. There's an excell wine list made up of bottles from both Europe and the New World. (☎070-345 85 87; www.restaurant raffles.nl; Javastraat 63; mains €18-25; ☺5.30-10pm Tue-Sat; ⚒; 🚃Javabrug)

Oker INTERNATIONAL €€

22 🍴 MAP P120, C2

Take your taste buds on a journey around the globe at perennially popular Oker. The menu of small plates draws on Italian, Japanese, Thai, French, Chinese and Lebanese cuisine for inspiration, and the list of wines by the glass is equally diverse. During 'oyster happy hour' (Saturday and Sunday between 4pm and 6pm), a plate of a dozen Fines de Claire oysters costs €15. (☎070-364 54 53; www.restaurantoker.nl; Denneweg 71; small plates €9-15; ☺11.30am-10pm Sun-Wed, to 11pm Thu-Sat; 🛜; 🚃Kuyperstraat)

Walter Benedict BISTRO €€

23 🍴 MAP P120, C2

All-day breakfasts (including a €5 coffee, juice and croissant deal) are on offer at this self-styled cafe-bistro, alongside lunch choices including soup, burgers and salads. Dinner is a mainly meaty affair – the steak served with smoked-garlic gravy and potatoes pan-fried in duck fat is renowned. (☎070-785 37 45; www.walterbene dict.nl; Denneweg 69a; breakfast dishes €3.50-11, lunch dishes €8-18, dinner mains €16-25; ☺9am-11pm; 🛜; 🚃Dr Kuyperstraat)

Madame Poulet CHICKEN €

24 🍴 MAP P120, A4

This lady sure knows how to roast a chicken. Free-range and raised without antibiotics, the juicy chickens are basted with aromatic herbs and roasted in a French Rotisol oven. Fresh side salads (Waldorf, bean, coleslaw or lentil) and *gratin dauphinois* (sliced potatoes baked with milk) are ordered separately. There are a few seats outside, but most regulars order to go. (www.madamepoulet.nl; Noordeinde 192; half/quarter chicken €8.75/4.75, sides €2.50-2.75; ☺4-9pm Mon & Tue, from 2pm Wed-Sun; 🚃Mauritskade)

Bloem CAFE €

25 🍴 MAP P120, D5

The rear salon in this cute cafe has a granny-style decor, replete with petit-point creations, knick-knacks and a floral carpet. It's a popular spot for afternoon high tea, and serves cakes, quiche and sandwiches at other times. (☎070-737 0589; www.bloemdenhaag.nl; Korte Houtstraat 6; sandwiches €6.50-7.50, cakes €3.50, high tea per person €20.50; ☺11am-4pm Tue, to 6pm Wed-Sun; 🚃Kalvermarkt-Stadhuis)

Het Heden CAFE €€

26 🍴 MAP P120, A4

The main draw here is the sunny rear garden, which is a lovely spot in which to enjoy a sandwich or *piadina* (Italian flatbread) lunch, a generous high tea or a simple dinner. The building, with its ornate brick exterior and stained-glass windows, dates from the 19th century and is one of the prettiest on Noordeinde. (☏ 070-346 46 64; https://hetheden.nl/; Noordeinde 148; sandwiches & piadini €5-10, high tea €20, dinner mains €18-24; ⏰ 11am-10pm Tue-Sat, to 5pm Sun; 🛜; 🚊 Mauritskade)

Zebedeüs

CAFE €€

27 ❌ MAP P120, B6

Abutting the walls of the Grote Kerk, Zebedeüs serves open sandwiches, toasties, pastas and soup all day, and a limited menu of more elaborate mains at night. Much of the produce used is organic. Cold-pressed raw veggie juices and freshly squeezed fruit juices are offered alongside coffee and alcohol. In fine weather, the best seats are at the chestnut-tree-shaded tables outside. (☏ 070-346 83 93; www.zebedeus.nl; Rond de Grote Kerk 8; sandwiches €7-9, pastas €10, dinner mains €21-24; ⏰ 11am-9.30pm; 🛜; 🚊 Gravenstraat, Grote Markt)

Mauritshuis Brasserie

BRASSERIE €

28 ❌ MAP P120, D5

More stylish than the average museum cafe, this brasserie in the Mauritshuis (p114) is a good choice for a coffee and pastry, light lunch or afternoon drink. (☏ 070-302 34 80; www.mauritshuis.nl/en/visit/plan-your-visit/brasserie/; Plein 29; sandwiches €9-10, pastry €4.50; ⏰ 12.30-6.30pm Mon, 9.30am-6.30pm Tue, Wed & Fri-Sun, 9.30am-8.30pm Thu; 🖍; 🚊 Centrum)

Vredespaleis (p123)

De Resident

DUTCH €€

29 MAP P120, C3

This local institution – here since 1977 – looks like something you might stumble upon in a Parisian back street. The elongated interior's red-leather booths, stained glass and old French advertising posters do nothing to shatter the illusion, nor does the menu of reliable bistro fare. There are very few vegetarian choices. (070-364 87 88; www.deresident.nl; Denneweg 58; mains €17-29; 5.30-10.30pm Mon-Sat, 5-9.30pm Sun)

Brasserie 't Ogenblik

CAFE €

30 MAP P120, B5

Staff zip about this hopping cafe at the nexus of several pedestrianised shopping streets; it also has some streetside tables along close-by Hoogstraat in summer. Coffees and teas offer refreshment, and a line-up of sandwiches, wraps, salads and soup offers sustenance. (070 365 64 54; www.t-ogenblik.nl; Molenstraat 4c; sandwiches €5-11, salads €12-14; 10am-5pm Mon-Fri, to 6pm Sat & Sun; ; Kneuterdijk)

Organic Farmers' Market

MARKET €

31 MAP P120, C6

Den Haag's organic farmers' market offers an array of local produce. (Hofweg; 10am-6pm Wed; Den Haag, Centrum)

Lola Bikes & Coffee

The owners and staff at much-loved **Lola** (Map p120, A4; www.facebook.com/LolaBikesandCoffee/; Noordeinde 91; 8am-6pm Tue-Sun; Mauritskade) are as passionate about cycling as they are about coffee, and their hybrid cafe and bike shop is testament to their passion. Racing bikes are repaired in a workshop at the rear, and excellent coffee and cake are served in the shabby-chic front space or cafe garden. It's also the home base of the Lola Cycling Club, which welcomes new members.

Drinking

Bouzy

WINE BAR

32 MAP P120, C2

On buzzing Denneweg, this sun-drenched corner bar has a wine list concentrating on European tipples but flirts with the New World too; there are dozens of bubbly varieties. Food choices include charcuterie and cheese platters, *flammkuchen* (Alsatian-style pizza) and the ubiquitous *bitterballen* (croquette balls). (070-780 35 63; www.bouzywine-andfood.nl; Denneweg 83; 3-11pm; Dr Kuyperstraat)

VaVoom!
COCKTAIL BAR

33 MAP P120, B7

Rum-based cocktails are the draw at this tiki bar in the city's major party precinct. An impressive 85 rums are available, and are used in knock-'em-dead concoctions such as the Jungle Jetsetter (Malibu rum, Maraschino cherry liqueur, lime and pineapple juice). (070-346 75 06; www.gmdh.nl/vavoom/; Grote Markt 29; 1pm-1am Mon-Wed & Sun, to 1.30am Thu-Sat)

De Paas
PUB

34 MAP P120, D8

A highly atmospheric old bar with a huge selection of Dutch, Belgian and other international beers, De Paas has 13 beers on tap, including unusual seasonal brews.

In summer, head to its floating terrace aboard a canal boat. (070-360 00 19; www.depaas.nl; Dunne Bierkade 16a; 4pm-1am Sun-Thu, 4pm-1.30am Fri, 3pm-1.30am Sat, 3pm-1am Sun;)

Café De Oude Mol
BROWN CAFE

35 MAP P120, B5

Pass through the ivy-covered door of Café de Oude Mol and you'll find this intimate, earthy pub that sums up the Dutch quality of *gezelligheid* (conviviality, cosiness). Live rock music takes to the stage on Mondays. Food is available from Wednesday to Saturday. (070-345 16 23; www.facebook.com/DeOudeMol/; Oude Molstraat 61; 5pm-1am Sun-Wed, to 2am Thu-Sat)

Gemeentemuseum (p122)

De Zwarte Ruiter
BROWN CAFE

6 MAP P120, B7

The Black Rider is a perennial Grote Markt favourite courtesy of its heated terrace and cavernous, light-filled, split-level interior. Live acts or DJs entertain the crowds on Friday and Saturday nights. (📞070-364 95 49; www.zmdh.nl/zwarte-ruiter/; Grote Markt 27; ⏰11am-1am Sun-Wed, to 1.30am Thu-Sat; 🚊Grote Markt)

Hometown Coffee & More
CAFE

37 MAP P120, C6

This on-trend cafe in the town centre has a street terrace from which you can watch shoppers saunter past and trams trundle by. Coffees range from the classic (espresso) to the faddish (turmeric, matcha, dirty chai) and food follows the same arc, with everything from sandwiches (€5 to €8) to açai bowls on the menu. (📞070-392 08 70; https://hometowncoffee.nl/; Buitenhof 4; ⏰9am-6pm Mon-Wed, 9am-8pm Thu-Sat, 10am-7pm Sun; 🚊Kneuterdijk)

Entertainment

Paard
LIVE MUSIC

38 ⭐ MAP P120, B7

Call it a club, a temple to live music or just a great place to hang out, Paard is a Den Haag institution. The program of live music is eclectic – everything from jazz to metal,

Spuiplein Precinct

From 2020, most headline cultural performances and events in Den Haag will be staged in a new complex in the Spuiplein precinct, located behind the Stadhuis in the city centre. The Nederlands Dans Theater, National Theatre (www.hnt.nl), Koninklijk Conservatorium (Royal Conservatory; www.koncon.nl) and Residentie Orkest (Philharmonic Orchestra; www.residentieorkest.nl) will all be based here.

blues, roots, reggae and soul – and festivals staged here include the Mondriaan Jazz Festival in October. Check the website for the program. (📞070-750 34 34; www.paard.nl; Prinsegracht 12; ⏰hrs vary; 🚊Grote Markt)

Nederlands Dans Theater
DANCE

39 ⭐ MAP P120, A5

This world-famous dance company has two main components: NDT1, the main company, and NDT2, a junior training division. The main company performs regularly in Den Haag, as well as internationally; tickets can be purchased through the website. Their (temporary) Den Haag homebase is at the Zuiderstrandtheater (p134). (www.ndt.nl; 🚊Statenlaan)

Filmhuis Den Haag
CINEMA

40 ⭐ MAP P120, D7

Screens foreign and indie films.
(📞070-365 60 30; www.filmhuisden
haag.nl; Spui 191; adult/student €8/7;
🚋Bierkade)

Zuiderstrandtheater

CONCERT VENUE

41 ⭐ MAP P120, A5

This performing arts theatre on
Scheveningen beach hosts jazz,
classical and pop concerts, as well
as dance performances. Check the
program on the website and book
tickets online or by telephone.
(South Beach Theatre; 📞070-880
03 33; www.zuiderstrandtheater.
nl; Houtrustweg 505, Vissershaven;
🚋Statenlaan)

Shopping

Mauritshuis Gift Shop
GIFTS & SOUVENIR

Classy souvenirs inspired by
works in the museum collection,
postcards, posters, books and
more are on offer at the excellent
Mauritshuis (p114) gift shop (see
28 ❌ Map p120, D5). (Plein 29; 🕐1-6pm
Mon, 10am-6pm Tue, Wed & Fri-Sun,
10am-8pm Thu; 🚋Centrum)

Frenken
CLOTHINC

42 🔒 MAP P120, A4

Saint Martins–trained Eric Frenken
was the head designer of women's
wear at Viktor & Rolf before
launching his own equally quirky
label. His beautifully tailored

Zuiderstrandtheater

eady-to-wear pieces are sold
at this sleek boutique on one of
the city's most alluring shopping strips. (www.frenkenfashion.
com; Noordeinde 113a; ◷noon-9pm
Thu, 10am-6pm Fri, 11am-6pm Sat;
▣Mauritskade)

Bookstor
BOOKS

43 🔒 MAP P120, B4

A hybrid cafe and second-hand
bookstore in Het Noordeinde
shopping area, this popular meeting spot offers coffee, pastries,
comfortable seating, chess sets
and lots of reading matter. Sit in
the bookshelf-lined main room, in
the rear garden or at a streetside
table. (📞070-326 57 90; Noordeinde
39; ◷9am-6pm; ▣Kneuterdijk)

Stanley & Livingstone
BOOKS

44 🔒 MAP P120, B6

Quaint travel bookshop with a
good range of guidebooks and
maps, as well as some travel accessories. (📞070-365 73 06; www.
stanley-livingstone.eu; Schoolstraat
21; ◷10am-6pm Tue, Wed & Fri, 10am-

Shopping Strips

Den Haag has plenty of
tempting shopping options,
with several great areas for
browsing. Grote Marktstraat is,
fittingly enough, where you'll
find the major department
stores and chains. Hoogstraat,
Noordeinde, Huelstraat and
Prinsestraat are lined with
boutiques and galleries.
Denneweg is celebrated not
only for its restaurants and
bars but also for its offbeat
boutiques.

9pm Thu, 10am-5pm Sat, 1-5pm Sun;
▣Grote Markt)

De Passage
MALL

45 🔒 MAP P120, C6

Entered from Spuistraat, Hofweg
or Gravenstraat, this elegant, 19th-
century covered arcade is home to
stores and cafes. (www.depassage.
nl; ◷noon-6pm Mon, 10am-6pm Tue,
Wed, Fri & Sat, 11am-5pm Sun)

Worth a Trip

Kinderdijk

Kinderdijk is a beautiful landscape of empty marshes and waterways above which 19 historic windmills (some brick, some timber) rise like sentinels. The mills are kept in operating condition and some still function as residences. In summer, tall reeds line the canals, lily pads float on the water and bird calls break the silence. It's a wonderful – and quintessentially Dutch – landscape to walk or bicycle through.

📞 078-691 28 30

www.kinderdijk.com

Nederwaard 1

admission free

🕐 site 24hr, museums & visitor centre 9am-5.30pm

🚤 Kinderdijk

History

The name Kinderdijk is said to derive from the horrible St Elizabeth's Day Flood of 1421 when a storm and flood washed a *kind* (child) in a crib up onto the dyke. Since that time, this part of the country has been a focus of Dutch efforts to claim land from the water. Several of the most important types of windmill are found here, including hollow post mills and rotating cap mills. The latter are among the highest in the country as they were built to better catch the wind.

What to See

The Kinderdijk site encompasses two canals, 19 traditional windmills, a historic pumping station that's been repurposed as a visitor centre and a dual pedestrian and bicycle path between the canals. Two of the windmills – the 17th-century Nederwaard and Blokweer mills – function as museums, offering an insight into the past lives of miller families. A video about the polder and its windmills screens in the pumping station. The walk or ride along the length of the site and back is an easy 5.7km. If you're lucky, some of the mills will have their sails spinning – a truly majestic sight. Entry to the canal path is free, but you'll need to purchase a ticket (adult/child 4–12 €8/5.50) to enter the two windmill museums and the visitor centre.

Exploring by Bike

The 28km **Kinderdijk Cycle Route** starts at the Kinderdijk Waterbus stop and follows the windmill-dotted southern bank of the Lek river to Bergstoep, before returning.

★ Top Tips

○ Bikes are carried on waterbuses for free.

○ The souvenir shop in front of the ferry dock hires bikes (€3 per hour).

○ The ticket to the windmill museums and visitor centre is €1 cheaper when booked online

✕ Take a Break

A simple cafe and ice-cream stands are dotted along the walking and cycling path. There's an old-fashioned cafe opposite the Water-bus stop, serving meals and weekend high teas.

★ Getting There

⚓ Waterbus fast ferry 202 from Eras-musbrug (adult/child €4/2, 30 minutes, eight daily). Direct ferries May to Octo-ber; at other times take a waterbus to Ridderkerk (adult/child €4/2, 30 min-utes, frequent) then another to Kinderdijk (adult/child €1.70, 10 minutes, frequent).

Worth a Trip 👀
Gouda

Gouda's association with cheese has made it famous – the town's namesake export is among the Netherlands' best known, and every Thursday in spring and summer the cheese market is held in front of the historic waag (weighing house). Other attractions include magnificent Sint Janskerk, an excellent museum and the beautiful Gothic Stadhuis (Town Hall; pictured), all within in Gouda's compact canal-ringed historic centre.

From Gouda's train station it's a five-minute walk to the centre of town.

Sint Janskerk

Impressive for its size (at 123m it's the longest church in the country) and its magnificent stained-glass windows, **Sint Janskerk** (0182-512 684; www.sintjan.com; Achter de Kerk 2; adult/student & child 13-18 €7/3.50; 9am-5pm Mon-Sat Mar-Oct, 10am-4pm Mon-Sat Nov-Feb) had chequered beginnings: previous incarnations of the building burned down with ungodly regularity every 100 years or so from 1361 until the mid-16th century, when the current structure was completed. A free audioguide gives loads of information about the 72 windows, which together form the largest cache of in-situ 16th-century stained glass in the world.

Museum Gouda

Housed in a medieval hospital building, the town's main **museum** (0182-33 10 00; www.museumgouda.nl; Achter de Kerk 14; adult/child 5-17 €10/4; 11am-5pm Tue-Sun) has a collection of artefacts and artworks related to Gouda and surrounding areas. There's plenty of *Gouds plateel* (glazed earthenware pottery), a collection of paintings by artists of the 19th-century Barbizon and Hague schools, a scale model of Gouda in 1562 and a ghoulish basement section on torture in the Middle Ages. The museum also hosts travelling and temporary exhibitions. There are entrances on Achter de Kerk and Oosthaven.

Stadhuis

Commanding attention in the middle of the Markt is this mid-15th-century **town hall** (088-000 15 05; www.stadhuysgouda.nl; admission €2.50; 10am-4pm Tue-Sat, 11am-4pm Sun Apr-Sep, 11am-3pm Tue-Sun Oct-Mar). Constructed from sandstone, this regal Gothic structure is testament to the wealth Gouda enjoyed from cloth trade. The ceremonial rooms are worth a look, but are often closed for private events. In winter, an ice-skating rink is built around Stadhuis.

★ Top Tips

○ There's a **tourist information desk** (VVV Gouda; 0182-589 110; www.welkomingouda.nl; Waag, Markt 35; 10am-5pm daily Apr-Oct, 10am-3pm Wed-Sun Nov-Mar) in the *waag*. Check the website for the many local events.

○ Buy the real deal in one of the many cheese shops. Try the aged Gouda, which can be hard to find outside the country.

✕ Take a Break

Have lunch at the museum's **cafe** (10am-5pm Tue-Sat, from 11am Sun); it has a gorgeous courtyard. Enjoy Gouda's other famous food, the *stroopwafel* (syrup waffle) at **Kamphuisen Siroopwafels** (0182-634 965; www.siroopwafelfabriek.nl; Markt 69; tour €9.95; 10am-6pm). For something a bit fancier, head to **Brunel** (0182-518 979; http://restaurantbrunel.nl; Hoge Grouwe 23; mains €19-21, set menus €27-30; 5-9.30pm Tue-Sat;).

Survival Guide

Luchtsingel (p59) MARKOV87/SHUTTERSTOCK ©

Before You Go

Book Your Stay

○ Accommodation options in Rotterdam are limited, though slowly expanding; as a result, it can sometimes be hard to find a room.

○ High season rates apply from April to September.

○ Book well in advance, especially during spring and summer.

○ Centrum is the most convenient option.

Useful Websites

Though accommodation options may be limited in Rotterdam, many travellers can find places to stay on the usual home-sharing services.

Lonely Planet (www. lonelyplanet.com/ the-netherlands/ rotterdam#lodgings) Recommendations and bookings.

Best Budget

King Kong Hostel (www.kingkonghostel

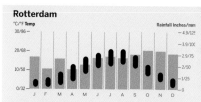

Rotterdam

°C/°F Temp — Rainfall inches/mm

When to Go

Summer The festival season kicks off and locals embrace outdoor activities; hotels charge high-season rates.

Autumn The weather remains pleasant and outdoor events are still held; be sure to pack an umbrella.

Winter Cold, but not bone-chilling. Low-season hotel rates apply.

Spring April and May are particularly good times to visit; lower chance of rain than at other times during the year.

.com) Bright and welcoming hostel on Rotterdam's main entertainment strip.

Stayokay Rotterdam (www.stayokay.com) Hostel located in the famous cube houses; offers basic rooms and a good cafe.

Best Midrange

Citizen M (www.citizen m.com) A hostel for grown ups; well-located.

Urban Residences (www.urbanresidences. com) Stylish, well-equipped apartments in the city centre.

Pincoffs (www. hotelpincoffs.nl) Rotterdam's only truly boutique hotel; strong on personalised service.

nhow (www.nhow -rotterdam.com) In the iconic De Rotterdam building; sleek rooms and a bar with panoramic terrace.

The James (https:// thejames.nl) Centrally located choice with good-sized, well-equipped rooms.

Best Top End

Mainport (www.main porthotel.com) Luxuri-

ous choice; loads of
facilities and excellent
riverside location.

Hotel New York (www.
hotelnewyork.nl) Bags
of character and very
friendly staff.

Arriving in Rotterdam

Centraal Station

Rotterdam's main
train station is **Rotterdam Centraal** (Map p38,
A1; www.ns.nl/stations
informatie/rtd/rotterdam-
centraal; Stationsplein 1;
Ⓜ Centraal Station,
🚊 Centraal); trains
heading south often
stop at Blaak Station
after Centraal.

From Brussels
Frequent high-speed
Thalys trains (1¼
hours), as well as NS
Intercity direct services
(two hours).

From Paris Thalys
trains travel to/from
Paris Nord (2½ hours).

The national railway
service **Nederlandse
Spoorwegen** (NS;
www.ns.nl) operates
trains to destinations
across the Nether-
lands, including Am-

sterdam (€15.40-17.80,
40 to 75 minutes).

Schiphol International Airport

The Netherlands' main
airport, **Schiphol** (AMS;
www.schiphol.nl) is lo-
cated 60km northeast
of Rotterdam. Airport
services include ATMs,
currency-exchange
desks, car-hire desks,
free wi-fi and multiple
eating and drinking
options.

Train Frequent Intercity
(€12.40, 45 minutes)
and Intercity Direct
(€14.80, 25 minutes)
trains travel between
the airport station and
Rotterdam Centraal.

Bus Interchange

Rotterdam is a hub for
Eurolines bus services
to the rest of Europe.
Long-distance buses
stop immediately
west of Centraal Sta-
tion. The **Eurolines
office** (📞 088 076 17
00; www.eurolines.eu/
rotterdam-eurolines-
agency; Conradstraat 16;
⏰ 9.30am-5.30pm Mon-
Sat; Ⓜ Centraal Station,
🚊 Centraal) is in the
Groothandelsgebouw
by Centraal Station.

Rotterdam The Hague Airport

Serving more than 40
(mainly European)
destinations, this
international airport
(RTM; 📞 010-446 34 44;
www.rotterdamthehagueair
port.nl; 🛜), 6km north-
west of Rotterdam, is
connected to the city
by bus or a combina-
tion of bus and metro.

Bus Bus 33 makes the
20-minute run between
the airport and Rot-
terdam Centraal Sta-
tion every 15 minutes
between 5.40am and
midnight (€3.50).

Bus & Metro Take
bus 33 to Meijersplein
metro station, then Line
E to Rotterdam; one
two-hour ticket (€3.50)
will cover both legs of
your trip.

Taxi The trip to get
to the centre takes
10 minutes and costs
around €25.

Getting Around

Metro

○ Excellent metro
system covering the city

Survival Guide Arriving in Rotterdam

Public Transport Tickets

Rotterdam's tram, bus and metro services are provided by RET (www.ret.nl). Most converge near Rotterdam Centraal Station. A RET information booth is located in the main entrance hall at Centraal Station and there are other information booths in the major metro stations; all sell tickets. These include the following.

Tourist Day Pass (€13.50) Unlimited travel on trams, buses, metro and Waterbus services.

One-Day RET Pass (€8) Allows travel on buses, trams and metro but not on Waterbus services.

Two-Hour Ticket (€3.50) Can be purchased from RET ticket offices, bus drivers and tram conductors; rechargeable at RET sales desks and reloading machines in metro stations.

OV Chipkaart (www.ret.nl/en/home/travel -products/public-transport-chip-card.html). If in the city for a few days, you'll save a lot of money by purchasing and charging one of these.

distance travelled, and cost between €4.50 and €10 per passenger; children under 13 travel half price.

○ See www.watertaxi rotterdam.nl for dock locations and zone information.

Essential Information

Accessible Travel

○ Download Lonely Planet's free Accessible Travel guides from http://lptravel.to/ AccessibleTravel.

○ Most offices and larger museums have lifts and/ or ramps, and accessible toilets.

○ Many budget and midrange hotels have limited accessibility, as they are in old buildings with steep stairs and no elevators.

○ Cobblestone streets (eg in Delft or Gouda) are rough for wheelchairs.

○ All train and metro stations in the city have wheelchair ramps, lifts and escalators.

and travelling as far as Den Haag.

○ Five lines (A, B, C, D and E); the major hubs are Beurs and Centraal Station.

○ Services operate from 5.30am (7.30am on Sunday) to 12.15am.

○ There's a metro map on the RET website (www.ret.nl).

Tram

○ An efficient way to get around, with nine lines traversing the city.

○ Services operate from 5am (from 7am on Sundays) to 12.30am.

Watertaxi

○ Small fast boats crisscross Nieuwe Maas river.

○ Tickets are charged by zone according to

- Most train stations and public buildings have accessible toilets.

- Buses have low boarding platforms for easy access.

- Some bus and tram stops have level-floor boarding.

- ANGO (☏033-465 43 43; www.ango.nl) is the Dutch national organisation for people with a disability.

Business Hours

Hours can vary by season and often decrease during the low season.

Banks 9am to 4pm Monday to Friday, some Saturday morning

Cafes and Bars Hours vary wildly

General Office Hours 8.30am to 5pm Monday to Friday

Museums 10am or 11am to 5pm daily, most close Monday

Restaurants Lunch noon to 2.30pm, dinner 6 to 10pm.

Shops 11am to 7pm Monday, 10am to 7pm Tuesday to Thursday, 10am to 9pm Friday, 10am to 7pm Saturday and noon to 7pm Sunday

Supermarkets 8am to 8pm; not all open on Sunday

Discount Cards

The **Rotterdam Welcome Card** (per adult 1/2/3 days €12/17/21) gives discounts of up to 50% on museum and attraction admission charges and food, as well as free public transport on RET metro, tram and bus services. You can purchase it online or at one of Rotterdam's tourist offices.

Electricity

Type C
230V/50Hz

Type F
230V/50Hz

Emergencies

Emergency ☏112

Police ☏0900 88 44

Fire department ☏010-446 89 00

LGBTI+ Travellers

There is a thriving LGBTI scene in Rotterdam. Many bars and clubs are found in the 'gay triangle' of the city, which is edged by Churchillplein, Westblaak, Mauritsweg and Van Oldebarneveldtstraat, near Eendrachtsplein metro station. The biggest event of the

LGBTI year is **Rotterdam Pride** (https://rotterdam-pride.com/en; ☉late Sep) in September. **Gay Rotterdam** (www.gayrotterdam.nl/en) is a useful resource.

Money

⊙ ATMs are widely available; some businesses don't accept credit or debit cards issued outside the Netherlands.

⊙ A growing number of businesses don't accept cash payments.

Tipping

The Dutch tip modestly and not always.
Hotel porters €1 to €2
Restaurants Round up, or 5%

PIN Only

A 'PIN only' sign signifies that the business doesn't accept cash payments. Be warned that it may not accept credit or debit cards issued outside the Netherlands either.

Public Holidays

Most museums adopt Sunday hours on public holidays (except Christmas and New Year, when they close) even if they fall on a day when the place would otherwise be closed, such as Monday. Many people treat Remembrance Day (4 May) as a day off.

Nieuwjaarsdag (New Year's Day) Parties and fireworks galore

Eerste Paasdag Easter Sunday

Tweede Paasdag Easter Monday

Koningsdag (King's Day) 27 April (26 April if the 27th is a Sunday)

Bevrijdingsdag (Liberation Day) 5 May; only an official holiday every five years

Hemelvaartsdag (Ascension Day) Fortieth day after Easter Sunday

Eerste Pinksterdag (Whit Sunday, Pentecost) Fiftieth day after Easter Sunday

Tweede Pinksterdag (Whit Monday) Fiftieth day after Easter Monday

Eerste Kerstdag (Christmas Day) 25 December

Tweede Kerstdag ('Second Christmas Day', aka Boxing Day) 26 December

Safe Travel

Crime and accident rates are relatively low in Rotterdam.

⊙ When walking through the city, be careful when crossing bike paths.

⊙ By law, police and regulatory bodies (eg bus and train conductors) are allowed to ask you for proof of ID; carry your passport or some official form of ID with you at all times.

⊙ Don't presume cars will stop for pedestrians at zebra crossings.

Taxes & Refunds

A value-added tax (VAT, or *BTW* in Dutch) rate of 21% is levied on most goods and services in the Netherlands. A 6% rate applies to food and drinks, books, pharmaceuticals, public transport, museum admissions and hotel rates.

Non-EU residents can claim a VAT refund on same-day purchases over €50; sales staff will provide documentation. Some department stores have dedicated VAT refund kiosks.

Dos & Don'ts

Pretty well anything goes here, although locals prize good manners (including queuing for entrance to public transport).

Holland v Netherlands Do not call the Netherlands 'Holland'; Holland comprises two provinces (Noord-Holland and Zuid-Holland) within the country.

Going Dutch When dining out, expect to pay your own way. Splitting the bill is common and no reason for embarrassment.

Straight talking Don't be offended if locals give you their frank, unvarnished opinion. It's not considered impolite, rather it comes from the desire to be direct and honest.

Telephone

The main Dutch phone network, KPN (www.kpn.com), is efficient, and prices are reasonable by European standards. The Netherlands uses the GSM mobile network. Buy a Dutch SIM card for your phone to avoid high roaming costs.

Country Code ☑31

Rotterdam area code ☑010

International access code ☑00

Mobile numbers These start with 06

Toll-free numbers These start with 0800

Toilets

○ There are public toilets (€0.70) on the upper floor of Centraal Station (p143).

○ The centrally located Bijenkorf Department Store (p43) has plenty of toilets.

○ You will need to pay around €0.50 for the use of most public toilets.

○ The app HogeNood (High Need; www. hogenood.nu) maps the nearest toilets based on your location, listing facilities in fast-food stores, department stores, public buildings, tourist offices and pubs.

Tourist Information

Main Rotterdam Tourist Office (Map p38, C3; ☑ 010-790 01 85; www. rotterdam.info; Coolsingel 114; ⊗ 9.30am-6pm; 🛜; Ⓜ Beurs) Offers maps, free wi-fi, brochures and advice about the city. Also has a gift shop (p53), 'Rotterdam Discovery' exhibition and garden cafe.

Tourist Information Desk, Rotterdam Centraal Station (Map p38, A1; www.rotterdam. info; Stationsplein 21, Centraal Station; ⊗ 9am-5.30pm Sun-Wed, 9am-8pm Thu-Sat mid-Aug–early Jul, 9am-7pm early Jul–mid-Aug) Located in the main station hall, next to the NS information desk. It provides maps and advice, and sells the Rotterdam Welcome Card (p145).

Tourist Information Point, Delft (Map p102, E3; ☑ 015-215 40 51; www. delft.com; Kerkstraat 3; ⊗ 11am-3pm Sun & Mon, 10am-4pm Tue-Sat) Supplies free town maps and runs a daily 90-minute guided walking tour (adult/child €5/free).

Tourist Office, Den Haag (VVV; Map p120, D6; 📞 070-361 88 60; www.denhaag.com; Spui 68; 🕐 noon-6pm Mon, 10am-6pm Tue-Fri, 10am-5pm Sat, noon-5pm Sun; 🚇; 🚊 Kalvermarkt-Stadhuis) Busy and helpful tourist office located on the ground floor of the public library in the landmark Stadhuis (Town Hall).

Visas

Tourists from nearly 60 countries – including Australia, Canada, Israel, Japan, New Zealand, Singapore, South Korea, the USA and most of Europe – need only a valid passport to visit the Netherlands for up to three months. EU nationals can enter for up to four months with a passport or national identity card.

Nationals of most other countries need a Schengen visa, valid within the EU member states (except the UK and Ireland), plus Norway and Iceland, for 90 days within a six-month period.

Language

The pronunciation of Dutch is fairly straightforward. If you read our coloured pronunciation guides as if they were English, you'll be understood just fine. Note that **öy** is pronounced as the 'er y' (without the 'r') in 'her year', and **kh** is a throaty sound, similar to the 'ch' in the Scottish *loch*. The stressed syllables are indicated with italics.

Where relevant, both polite and informal options in Dutch are included, indicated with 'pol' and 'inf' respectively.

To enhance your trip with a phrasebook, visit lonelyplanet. com. Lonely Planet iPhone phrasebooks are available through the Apple App store.

Basics

Hello.	*Dag./Hallo.*	dakh/ ha·loh
Goodbye.	*Dag.*	dakh
Yes.	*Ja.*	yaa
No.	*Nee.*	ney

Please.
Alstublieft. (pol)   al·stew·bleeft
Alsjeblieft. (inf)   a·shuh·bleeft

Thank you.
Dank u/je. (pol/inf)   dangk ew/yuh

Excuse me.
Excuseer mij.   eks·kew·zeyr mey

How are you?
Hoe gaat het   hoo khaat huht
met u/jou? (pol/inf)   met ew/yaw

Fine. And you?
Goed. En met   khoot en met
u/jou? (pol/inf)   ew/yaw

Do you speak English?
Spreekt u   spreykt ew
Engels?   eng·uhls

I don't understand.
Ik begrijp   ik buh·khreyp
het niet.   huht neet

Eating & Drinking

I'd like ...
Ik wil graag ...   ik wil khraakh ...

a beer	*een bier*	uhn beer
a coffee	*een koffie*	uhn ko·fee
a table	*een tafel*	uhn taa·fuhl
for two	*voor twee*	vohr twey
the menu	*een menu*	uhn me·new

I don't eat (meat).
Ik eet geen (vlees).
ik eyt kheyn (vleys)

Delicious!
Heerlijk!/Lekker!   heyr·luhk/le·kuhr

Cheers!
Proost!   prohst

Please bring the bill.
Mag ik de   makh ik duh
rekening   rey·kuh·ning
alstublieft?   al·stew·bleeft

Shopping

I'd like to buy ...
Ik wil graag ... kopen.
ik wil khraakh ... koh·puhn

I'm just looking.
Ik kijk alleen maar.
ik keyk a·leyn maar

How much is it?
Hoeveel kost het?
hoo·veyl kost huht

That's too expensive.
Dat is te duur.
dat is tuh dewr

Can you lower the price?
Kunt u wat van de prijs afdoen?
kunt ew wat van duh preys af·doon

Emergencies

Help!
Help!   help

Call a doctor!
Bel een dokter!
bel uhn dok·tuhr

Call the police!
Bel de politie!
bel duh poh·leet·see

I'm sick.
Ik ben ziek.
ik ben zeek

I'm lost.
Ik ben verdwaald.
ik ben vuhr·dwaalt

Where are the toilets?
Waar zijn de toiletten?
waar zeyn duh twa·le·tuhn

Time & Numbers

What time is it?
Hoe laat is het?
hoo laat is huht

It's (10) o'clock.
Het is (tien) uur.
huht is (teen) ewr

Half past (10).
Half (elf).
half (elf) (lit: half eleven)

morning	*'s ochtends*	sokh·tuhns
afternoon	*'s middags*	smi·dakhs
evening	*'s avonds*	saa·vonts

yesterday	*gisteren*	khis·tuh·ruhn
today	*vandaag*	van·daakh
tomorrow	*morgen*	mor·khuhn

1	*één*	eyn
2	*twee*	twey
3	*drie*	dree
4	*vier*	veer
5	*vijf*	veyf
6	*zes*	zes
7	*zeven*	zey·vuhn
8	*acht*	akht
9	*negen*	ney·khuhn
10	*tien*	teen

Transport & Directions

Where's the ...?
Waar is ...?
waar is ...

How far is it?
Hoe ver is het?
hoo ver is huht

What's the address?
Wat is het adres?
wat is huht a·dres

Can you show me (on the map)?
Kunt u het mij tonen (op de kaart)?
kunt ew het mey toh·nuhn (op duh kaart)

A ticket to ..., please.
Een kaartje naar ..., graag.
uhn kaar·chuh naar ... khraakh

Please take me to ...
Breng me alstublieft naar ...
breng muh al·stew·bleeft naar ...

Does it stop at ...?
Stopt het in ...?
stopt huht in ...

I'd like to get off at ...
Ik wil graag in ... uitstappen.
ik wil khraak in ... öyt·sta·puhn

Can we get there by bike?
Kunnen we er met de fiets heen?
ku·nuhn wuh uhr met duh feets heyn

Behind the Scenes

Send Us Your Feedback

We love to hear from travellers – your comments help make our books better. We read every word, and we guarantee that your feedback goes straight to the authors. Visit **lonelyplanet.com/contact** to submit your updates and suggestions.

Note: We may edit, reproduce and incorporate your comments in Lonely Planet products such as guidebooks, websites and digital products, so let us know if you don't want your comments reproduced or your name acknowledged. For a copy of our privacy policy visit lonelyplanet.com/privacy.

Virginia's Thanks

In the Netherlands, many thanks to Kim Heinen, Annemieke Loef, Renske Satijn, Nina Swaep and Eveline Zoutendijk. At LP's London office, thanks to Dan Fahey and Jennifer Carey. At home in Melbourne, thanks and much love to Peter and Max Handsaker.

Acknowledgements

Cover photograph: Cube houses, Overblaak Development, Francesco Carovillano/4Corners ©

Photographs p8, top: www.designJAAP.com; p30: Iris van den Broek;Victor Maschek;Evgeny Prokofyev;Peppermint Joe/Shutterstock ©; p96: Tom Goossens;Frank Cornelissen/Shutterstock ©

This Book

This first edition of Lonely Planet's *Pocket Rotterdam* guidebook was researched, written and curated by Virginia Maxwell. This guidebook was produced by the following:

Destination Editor
Daniel Fahey

Senior Product Editor
Genna Patterson

Regional Senior Cartographer
Mark Griffiths

Product Editor
Barbara Delissen

Cartographer Alison Lyall

Book Designer
Gwen Cotter

Assisting Editor
Fionnula Twomey

Cover Researcher
Naomi Parker

Thanks to Janice Bird, Hannah Cartmel

index

See also separate subindexes for:

Eating p154

Drinking p154

Entertainment p155

Shopping p155

Sights 000
Map Pages **000**

LONELY PLANET <small>IN THE</small> WILD

Send your 'Lonely Planet in the Wild' photos to social@lonelyplanet.com
We share the best on our Facebook page every week!

Our Writer

Virginia Maxwell

Although based in Australia, Virginia spends at least half of her year updating Lonely Planet destination coverage across the globe. The Mediterranean is her major area of interest – she has covered Spain, Italy, Turkey, Syria, Lebanon, Israel, Egypt, Morocco and Tunisia – but she also covers Finland, Bali, Armenia, the Netherlands, the US and Australia for Lonely Planet products. Follow her @maxwellvirginia on Instagram and Twitter.

31901064641865

Published by Lonely Planet Global Limited
CRN 554153
1st edition – May 2019
ISBN 978 1 78701 796 2
© Lonely Planet 2019   Photographs © as indicated 2019
10 9 8 7 6 5 4 3 2 1
Printed in Malaysia